Gaming the Past

Despite the growing number of books designed to radically reconsider the educational value of video games as powerful learning tools, there are very few practical guidelines conveniently available for prospective history and social studies teachers who actually want to use these teaching and learning tools in their classes. As the games and learning field continues to grow in importance, *Gaming the Past* helps social studies teachers and teacher educators implement this unique and engaging new pedagogy. It focuses on specific examples to help social studies educators effectively use computer·simulation games to teach critical thinking and historical analysis. Chapters cover the core parts of conceiving, planning, designing, and implementing simulation based lessons.

Additional topics include:

- Talking to colleagues, administrators, parents, and students about the theoretical, practical, and educational value of using historical simulation games
- Selecting simulation games that are aligned to curricular goals
- Determining hardware and software requirements, purchasing software, and preparing a learning environment that can incorporate simulations
- Planning lessons and implementing instructional strategies
- Identifying and avoiding common pitfalls
- Developing activities and assessments for use with simulation games that facilitate the interpretation and creation of established and new media

Gaming the Past also includes sample unit and lesson plans, worksheets, and suggestions for further reading. The book ends with brief profiles of the majority of historical simulation games currently available freely on the Internet and from commercial vendors.

Jeremiah McCall, Ph.D., teaches secondary history at Cincinnati Country Day School. He has been involved in the study and use of simulation games in history education for nearly a decade and is a frequent presenter on the topic at teaching conferences including *Education Arcade* and *Games and Learning Society*.

Gaming the Past

Using Video Games to Teach Secondary History

Jeremiah McCall

Routledge
Taylor & Francis Group

NEW YORK AND LONDON

First published 2011
by Routledge
52 Vanderbilt Avenue, New York, NY 10017

Simultaneously published in the U.K.
by Routledge
2 Park Square, Milton Park, Abingdon, Oxon OX14 4RN

Routledge is an imprint of the Taylor & Francis Group, an informa business

© 2011 Taylor & Francis

The right of Jeremiah McCall to be identified as author of this work
has been asserted by him in accordance with sections 77 and 78
of the Copyright, Designs and Patents Act 1988.

Library of Congress Cataloging in Publication Data
McCall, Jeremiah B., 1972–.
  Gaming the past: using video games to teach secondary history/
Jeremiah McCall.
    p. cm.
  1. History—Study and teaching—Simulation methods.
  2. Video games—Study and teaching.   I. Title.
  D16.255.S5M37 2011
  907.1′2—dc22   2011000556

ISBN13: 978–0–415–88759–5 (hbk)
ISBN13: 978–0–415–88760–1 (pbk)
ISBN13: 978–0–203–83183–0 (ebk)

Typeset in Bembo and Helvetica Neue by
Florence Production Ltd, Stoodleigh, Devon

For Olivia

Contents

Illustrations

TABLES

FIGURES

BOXES

Acknowledgements

This book is the culmination, though not by any means the end, of a journey begun more than a decade ago to develop effective classroom uses of historical simulations. So many people have had a hand in this journey, not least of all my parents, siblings, teachers, and friends. There are too many to name, but I will, nonetheless, name a few.

It was early 2005 when I had the good fortune to meet Kurt Squire. He is an educational visionary and his work in the field of games and learning has served as a model to all who engage these issues. He heard of my early experiments with *Civilization* in the classroom and graciously invited me to share my experiences at the 2005 Education Arcade in Los Angeles. Since then Kurt's great generosity and support—inviting me to conferences, responding encouragingly to my many emails, and even steering reporters my way—brought my ideas to a larger audience and made me aware that they were worth sharing in the first place. For all this, I owe Kurt a great debt of gratitude.

I also want to thank the editors at Routledge, Kim Guinta and Catherine Bernard, who saw the merit in this book and found it a home even though it was not quite like anything that had come before. My thanks also go to Georgette Enriquez, who helped me navigate the intricacies of the publication process.

I am grateful to have taught history at Cincinnati Country Day School for the past eight years. Here in what I truly believe is one of the finest schools in the world, I have had the encouragement and support of friends and colleagues to grow continuously as a teacher. Special thanks belong to my good friend and colleague, Greg Martin. His tireless enthusiasm for the promise of simulation-based learning, and indeed all manifestations of effective twenty-first-century pedagogy, is inspiring. We share a vision of how formal education can still be and that has made my work so much more meaningful. His support has helped make this book far better, though of course any remaining flaws are wholly my own. Finally, I cannot leave the topic of CCDS without expressing my deepest thanks to my students. They are my inspiration and my source of energy day in and out, the main reason I do what I do as a teacher.

Last, but most important of all, are my thanks to my wife, Olivia. Beyond her love and support in this and all the endeavors I undertake, her ability to keep me balanced over the years has meant more than text can ever express. Being with her has made academic accomplishments like this worth doing while reminding me that walking in parks, bright autumn leaves, and so many other things are equally worthwhile. Thank you, Olivia.

Introduction

The Power of Simulation Games

Simulation games can model complex real-world relationships and systems in ways that are nearly impossible for static words and images. Consider, on any given day in a history class a teacher or text could declare something like, "Throughout the past, resources have been scarce and finite. This has meant that societies, historically, have had to make often difficult choices about how best to allocate resources. Societies had to make trade-offs between conflicting goals." Reading or hearing this is a very different experience from dealing with the reality of such trade-offs in a computer simulation game like, say, *Civilization*. Each city in that game has a labor force that can exploit resources from one of the squares of the land surrounding the city and, in doing so, add to the economic, scientific, and productive efforts of the city. The more citizens a city has, generally speaking, the more productive the city is. There are consequences, however, to building a city's population. Larger populations experience greater unhappiness due to overcrowding among other issues. If the level of unhappiness in the city is greater than the level of happiness, one or more citizens will refuse to work in protest of the situation. These unhappy citizens produce nothing but continue to consume resources such as food (see Figure I.1).

Left unchecked, unhappy citizens can severely hamper a city's ability to build, research, and generate revenue. Any attempt to address the problem of unhappiness in a city, however, will require a sacrifice of some sort. The player can increase the proportion of his civilization's tax revenues spent on luxuries to make more unhappy citizens happy or try to prevent unhappiness in the first place. Increased spending on luxuries means decreased spending elsewhere. So the research of gunpowder may take longer than planned, perhaps, or the savings to construct an important temple will need to be tapped because the higher spending on luxuries

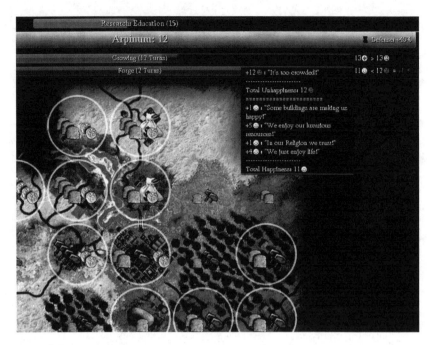

Figure I.1 Firaxis' *Civilization IV*: happiness levels in a city
Credit: © Firaxis Games

has created a budget deficit. The simulation game has modeled the multifaceted complexity of scarcity where the words describe in a static and linear fashion.

To take a second example, consider some of the assertions a text or teacher might make during a study of presidential politics.

- "A common criticism of presidential candidates in general elections is that they are not completely truthful and completely consistent in the views they present while campaigning."
- "Another criticism sometimes made of presidential campaigns is that the money a candidate has available for campaigning is too important a factor in their success. It would be extremely difficult, if not impossible, for a citizen of modest resources to win the presidency."

Hearing or reading these static declarations is very different from experiencing them in a simulation game like *Political Machine*. In this particular game the player manages the U.S. presidential campaign for Barack Obama or John McCain, or, alternatively, a hypothetical campaign for other contemporary politicians ranging from Hillary Clinton to Mitt

Romney. Play centers on sending the candidate to various states to make political speeches and advertisements addressing the concerns of voters. Like most effective simulation games, players of *Political Machine* (Figure I.2) cannot do everything or be everywhere at once and must choose between conflicting options. Players in this game are strictly limited in what they can do any particular turn. For practical purposes, candidates can only campaign in one or two states per turn, and advertising and traveling costs money. Successful candidates must be selective in the states they frequent and the messages they stress.

Given these limitations, which correspond to the reality of modern presidential campaigns, a highly efficient campaign strategy is to visit key states and simply issue speeches and ads that tell the people of the state what they want to hear—in other words it is possible to win the game by following the polls rather than crafting a coherent principled platform. Money is also a critical factor in these games. Traveling, hiring staff, constructing headquarters, and placing ads all cost money. A player who does not address fundraising regularly and manage campaign funds with some responsibility will find her campaign stalled before the elections. Again, the simulation game offers direct analogies to the practical realities of the campaign trail.

Figure I.2 Stardock's *The Political Machine*
Credit: © Stardock Systems Inc.

Civilization and *Political Machine* are just two of the many examples of historical simulation games, the topic of this book. The term simulation is used to refer to a variety of things, including business training games, flight simulators, and even weather prediction software. In its broadest sense, a simulation is a working dynamic model that is designed to represent one or more aspects of the real world in a simplified way. Games, too, are defined in a variety of ways. A useful working definition that this book will follow can be paraphrased from Salen and Zimmerman (2003): a game is a rule-based system in which players undergo a conflict or competition in an attempt to achieve a quantifiable goal, such as winning or losing (80). A simulation game, then, is a game that functions as a dynamic model of one or more aspects of the real world.

If you are reading this book, you are open to the power of computer-based simulation games as learning tools in the social studies. You are open to becoming part of what will likely prove to be a critical development in twenty-first-century education. The potential of video games, and indeed of play itself, to provide rich learning opportunities has become an important topic in current debates about education. Within debates to rethink traditional ideas about education and learning and recast educational practices to meet the needs of twenty-first-century learners, some theorists have advocated that play, far from being merely frivolous, can provide deep, meaningful learning experiences, and develop creative thinking in ways unachievable by traditional pedagogies alone. Still others have focused on the power of video games, specifically, as tools for deep learning, planting the seeds for new fields of study devoted to the intersection of games and learning. James Gee is one of the pioneers in this area, whose work has laid a foundation for the study of video games and learning. Gee, and subsequent writers, have noted that games, with their multimodal appeal to the senses, are more than simply entertainment. Successful commercial games incorporate sound principles of learning within the designs, and this is a fundamental part of their ability to engage players. Ranging from lightning-fast racing games, to duels with extraterrestrial invaders, puzzles, pet owner simulations, and city builders, games appeal to the desire to solve problems. They invite players to sample different identities, and navigate new worlds, take risks and explore possibilities that would be difficult to entertain easily in the physical world. Scholarship has burgeoned in the wake of Gee's work. The number of books and articles dealing with the theoretical potential of games as learning tools in the context of instructional design and educational psychology is already substantial. So too is the literature devoted to analyzing games as sets of rules, forms of narrative, entirely new species of media, or something in between. Academic programs in game studies are developing; specialized departments have sprung up, at the University of Wisconsin, MIT, and other institutions. National conferences on the power of games and learning have sprung up; the University of Wisconsin–Madison's Games Learning and Society Conference, now in its sixth year in 2010, allows academic researchers, game developers, and educators to meet and share ideas on the power of games as learning tools that can shape society.

These ideas are penetrating into high school and college classrooms in formal ways slowly. Beyond the independent initiatives of classroom teachers who have effectively employed games in the classroom for years, the Quest 2 Learn School in New York was launched in 2009, a 6–12th grade school with a game-based learning curriculum. Nevertheless, despite the increasing reconsideration of the educational value of play, and the growing view of games as powerful twenty-first-century learning tools, there are very few practical guidelines conveniently available for pre-service teachers—indeed for any educators—who actually want to use video games as teaching and learning tools in their classes. There are a few scattered, helpful resources on the Internet, to be sure, but those who want a thorough introduction to the topic, a structured approach and concrete set of classroom uses for video games, are still essentially left with very few options. This situation needs to be remedied. The ideas of the researchers and theorists show great promise, but, for those ideas to reach fruition, more must be done to create and share specific practical implementations of game-based learning for those who will teach in the classrooms of tomorrow.

This book is intended to help address the imbalance between theory and practice primarily for the benefit of pre-service history and social studies teachers of middle school, high school, and college students. Practicing teachers interested in exploring in detail the effective use of simulation games will also find this book helpful. It is a guide to selecting computer-based historical simulation games, planning instructional strategies and assessments, and implementing simulation-centered lessons to enhance the studies of history and social studies students.

Before beginning, a few more comments on the aims and content of this book are warranted. The first is a note on the word "historical" in historical simulation games. The primary focus of this book is on simulation games that deal with the past. In practice the line between the past and present is very blurry, particularly for historians of the recent past. This is certainly the case with middle and high school history classes. Social studies educators teaching history classes regularly find themselves, rightly, drawing connections between past and present to students. Many history classes themselves are designed to extend into the very recent past of the last few years. Furthermore, one person may consider *Third World Farmer*, a portrayal of modern subsistence farming in developing nations, to be a current events game. Another, however, may note that the problems facing subsistence farmers in developing nations have existed for decades or more, and thus judge *Third World Farmer* to be a historical simulation. Since the goal of this book is to provide as much assistance to those planning to teach history and social studies as possible, the term historical simulation game is used to encompass all games that portray the past, whether that past is 1 year old or 1,000 years old. Some are also included that consider future issues like sources of energy and global warming that are, like all future issues, rooted in past issues that fall under the purview of history.

Second, though this text is certainly informed by research and theory on historical cognition, games and learning, and formal game analysis, it does not include lengthy discussions of that theory. This has already been done in print elsewhere a number of times, and the purpose of this book is to implement more than it is to add to the theory of games and learning or re-establish the theoretical underpinnings of history education per se— though it does make the case that historical simulation games should be treated as interpretations of the past that should be analyzed using valid historical methods. Readers who want to investigate existing work on games and learning, historical cognition and history pedagogy, and formal game analyses, will find numerous suggestions for further reading in Appendix D.

Rather than focus on adding to theory, this text guides pre-service and active teachers who want to develop specific, effective classroom applications of historical simulation games. As the games and learning field continues to grow in importance, trainers of new teachers will need texts like this to help train their students in this twenty-first-century pedagogy before they enter the classroom. The core parts of conceiving, planning, designing, and implementing simulation-based lessons are treated:

- Talking to colleagues, administrators, parents, and students about the theoretical and practical educational value of using historical simulation games.
- Selecting simulation games that are aligned to curricular goals from the variety of available history-themed games.
- Planning lessons and implementing instructional strategies.
- Developing activities and assessments for use with simulation games that facilitate the interpretation and creation of established and new media.

These topics are supplemented by sample worksheets, suggestions for crafting rubrics, and lesson templates that can be used and modified for current and future games. At the end comes a substantial appendix with brief overviews for the majority of historically themed simulation games available as standalone and web browser-based programs on Windows® PCs—and whenever available, on Macs. Additional appendices deal with determining hardware and software requirements and purchasing software; suggest some important Internet sources for documents and studies that can aid students in analyzing simulations; and provide suggestions for further reading. Equipped with the guidance from this book, pre-service and in-service teachers will be well prepared to develop engaging and effective simulation-based lessons that encourage students to develop their skills as historians, systems-thinkers, and critics of twenty-first-century media.

CHAPTER 1

Why Play Historical Simulation Games?

Making the Case to Administrators, Parents, Colleagues, and Students

O ur survey begins with a fundamental question: Why should simulation games be employed in history classes? Though there are many supporters of this learning tool, there are also a fair number of parents, administrators, fellow teachers, and, yes, even students who will need to be persuaded, or at least made more comfortable with the value of simulation games as learning tools. This next section offers a set of important talking points to use with these various groups when discussing simulations. Equipped with such reasons teachers can advocate the value of simulation games in their own schools and articulate persuasively the benefits to students, colleagues, administrators, and parents.

Since it is, after all, history and social studies education that is the concern of this book, it is important to begin by considering the educational philosophy for teaching history. This philosophy provides the solid foundation for using simulation games.

WHAT IS IT WE TEACH WHEN WE TEACH HISTORY?

The path to understanding the importance of video games as learning tools in history education needs to be approached by briefly critiquing the conventional wisdom concerning history education and clarifying the role and objectives of the history teacher. It is all too clear that many students of history classes—and judging from those students' experiences some who teach it—operate according to a belief that history is no more than the established record of past events and their causes, fixed by the professionals, and received by everyone else. Viewing history this way can only lead students to an unfortunate habit of intellectual passivity. They will learn to surrender their right to reason and be taught that only the authorities have the right to think and speak about the world—why it is the way it is.

This is not only unhelpful for students of history and social studies, it is simply incorrect. For the expert practitioners, history is the act of constructing meaningful, critically researched and validated interpretations of the past, interpretations focused on human motivations, actions, and the effects of those actions. It is a discipline, and those who practice in the discipline, historians, are in the business of rigorously sifting through evidence, drawing connections, and constructing defensible explanations and interpretations of past human actions, their causes, and their effects. Though these efforts are governed by critical methodologies—those of source criticism, and creating and testing defensible models of human behavior among others—there is no pretense among historians that complete objectivity is possible. The cherished ideal once held centuries ago that an objective factual past could be accurately recorded and reported as it really was by the impartial historian is long gone. Modern historians engage in a more Sisyphean task. They must strive to interpret the past as objectively and accurately as possible, knowing, however, that their interpretations cannot be anything more than provisional, influenced by their assumptions and preferences and subject to rejection by future historians with different assumptions and evidence.

This past decade, the importance of teaching students how experts in a discipline solve problems has become an important goal in all branches of middle and secondary education. For history and social studies classes, teaching students to view history and the social sciences as disciplines requires that teachers move far beyond promoting rote memorization and train students to evaluate evidence, engage in meaningful discussions, form their own valid interpretations of the past, and offer valid criticisms of others' interpretations. This sort of training provides students with a far richer understanding of the past, and better training in critical thinking skills, than an approach encouraging students merely to learn the interpretations of others. Reinforcing the point, students who learn to engage in historical research, reconstruction, and argument experience a richer, more meaningful, and more beneficial education than those who are taught that history is no more than a set of fixed events, causes, and effects that simply must be learned and recalled on demand. To gain skill as a historian requires gaining the ability to:

- Pose meaningful questions about the peoples of the past.
- Evaluate sources and analyze the evidence they provide about the past.
- Discriminate between the essential and trivial components of a historical event, its potential causes, and its effects.
- Analyze dynamic systems: the interrelationships between humans, humans and the environment, and how these relationships influence human actions.
- Adopt, in order to gain insight, the perspective of individuals from the past.
- Combine pieces of evidence into plausible interpretations of the past that offer clear considerations of potential causes and effects and are situated in historical contexts.

These skills are complemented by the understanding that all reconstructions of the past are interpretations: provisional, standing or falling on the strength of their evidence and arguments, subject to revisions, and very much dependent on the historians who create them. Trained to view and practice history this way, students can come to appreciate the discipline of history as a lens through which they can view the world. They learn to "do" history by forming their own justifiable conclusions about the past. In the process, students learn fundamental skills of analysis, interpretation, critique, and synthesis that will serve them well.

TALKING POINT: THE REQUIREMENTS OF HISTORY EDUCATION IN THE TWENTY-FIRST CENTURY

Analyzing and critiquing interpretations of the past, reconstructions of how and why things happened, whether that past is a day, century, or millennium ago, are among the most vital skills that history and social science education can foster in a twenty-first-century learner. In a world with so many completing claims to truth and such decentralization of information throughout the Internet, students need, more than ever, to be able to evaluate the plausibility of others' interpretations of how and why the world works the way it does. To do so requires examining the underlying evidence supporting an interpretation. It also requires scrutinizing the assumptions of the author—in this context the creator of text, sound, or image—and the relationship between different parts of the interpretation. To this end, it is critical that students examine historical evidence directly through its original sources. In other words, they should read the writings and view the images produced by the societies they study, and learn to critique the credibility of those who created the works. Further, they must strive to appreciate the great differences in material circumstances and worldviews that underpin these authors' accounts, contextualizing authors' testimonies within the worlds in which they lived. Considering how they and others know what they know is part and parcel of building and critiquing interpretations of the past.

The fundamentals of critiquing sources, unearthing hidden assumptions, and appreciating contexts and relationships, have always been a critical part of the historian's training. The twenty-first-century learner, however, faces a daunting array of new media types, and variations on each type. The number of media types will only increase over time. In response to the proliferation of new media, the (U.S.) National Council of Social Studies and the National Council of Teachers of English have crafted position statements identifying twenty-first-century media literacy skills as a critical component of education in these disciplines. These standards suggest that our students, in addition to the established need to critique established oral, print, and visual sources of information, need to be skilled critics and careful users of information in a variety of newer forms, including: simulation software; television and video; wikis and other online visual and textual sources; and multimedia. Furthermore, students should be able to publish their opinions and reasoned findings using a variety of media, including: wikis, blogs, video, graphics, and multimedia presentation software. These recommendations are connected philosophically to the concern that the future belongs to those who can best analyze, create, and design, not just compile information.

Advocates for educational reform generally agree that the core skills for the new millennium include:

- creative, imaginative, flexible, and innovative thought, which includes the ability to develop good questions;
- effective collaboration;
- the discipline and motivation to acquire deep knowledge of a domain;
- the ability to synthesize effectively from a variety of sources and materials.

The term "right-brained thinking" is often used to symbolize learners who tap fully into their creative, productive, and innovative side to approach problems from new angles and develop new solutions. When so many of the skilled jobs in the twentieth-century economy can be performed by less expensive and equally capable workforces outside the United States, some theorists say, those who can move beyond the winning skill sets of the last century will have the greatest professional opportunities. So, the game designers and artists will be more important than the coders, the expert diagnosticians than the x-ray readers, the news analysts than the news aggregators, and so on. Traditional education, following the argument of educational revisionists, must be transformed to prepare today's learners for the new ways of the world. This is especially true of those traditional educational practices that have stifled, rather than promoted, creativity, undermined teamwork to promote competition between individuals, and trained students using only techniques that, for the most part, have not changed in any substantial way for centuries: the lecture and the Socratic discussion.

Fostering flexible, nimble, creative, curious, and collaborative student-thinkers who can criticize digital sources as easily as textual ones, analyze systems, construct defensible explanations of how and why human societies function the way they do, and evaluate interpretations and models—this is the goal of twenty-first-century history and social studies teachers. It is no small task, but simulation games can serve as a critical learning tool to assist teachers in this challenge. The remaining talking points elaborate on the benefits of simulation games as tools for twenty-first-century history and address possible concerns about the richness of a lesson incorporating simulation games.

The conception of effective twenty-first-century history education laid out in these two talking points serves as the foundation for talking to students, parents, and administrators about the importance of simulation games. The talking points in the remainder of the chapter rest upon this foundation.

TALKING POINT: SIMULATIONS ARE SUPERIOR TOOLS FOR LEARNING ABOUT HISTORICAL CONTEXT, HISTORICAL SYSTEMS, AND HISTORICAL LIMITATIONS

Simulation games are exceptionally well suited to the promotion of historical questions, study of historical systems, building of real-world contexts, and development of a level of understanding for the contexts in which people of the past lived. These are perhaps their most significant contributions to the history class. Students at all levels, and even teachers of history, can forget that the people of the past lived and operated in a multitude of physical, spatial, and intellectual systems, all of which provided the context for their lives and actions. They had to get food, walk places, and satisfy basic needs and comforts. They lived within a world of beliefs and practices shaped by their culture and communities. All of these factors affected individuals' ideas and actions. It is too easy, unfortunately, to divorce the people of the past from their physical, spatial, and cultural contexts. This can be done just as readily by treating history as purely literary exercise, conducted solely through reading and writing, as it can by presenting it as an exercise in rote learning where events and dates are severed from their contexts. If the study of the past is to help us understand motivations, actions, and consequences, teachers of history need to seize opportunities to make the past come alive for students, to place documents, images, and facts within a living context.

Simulation games help remedy this forgetfulness of context and of the functioning systems that encompassed the people of the past. Their effectiveness in this realm makes studying simulation games more than simply a legitimate option for a lesson design; there are concepts and situations within social studies education that call explicitly for the educational advantages of a simulation game. The understanding of systems and contexts essential to historical interpretation that a historical simulation game can generate goes beyond that created by many other kinds of secondary sources. This is more than a matter of engagement, though game-based exercises are often highly engaging. It is a matter of putting students into dynamic recreations of roles and situations from the past. A simulation can place students at the center of complex systems where a variety of variable factors ebb and flow simultaneously in ways that cannot be readily represented in other media.

The principle is straightforward: to analyze a system, use a roughly analogous, but simplified, model of the system, a simulation game. Simulation games, when carefully chosen and effectively used, offer unique learning opportunities. A simulation game is a simplified virtual system that models a vastly more complicated historical system. Playing such a game is, essentially, manipulating a system. There is a direct analogy between the components of an effective simulation game and the components of the real world it represents. The food production system in *CivCity: Rome*, for example, has real-world analogies in the ancient Mediterranean. The impact of a tsunami on shore barriers in *Stop Disasters* has a real-world analogy in the monstrous waves of the Pacific. The ability of random acts of violence to degrade peace talks between Palestinians and Israelis in *Peacemaker* reflects a real-world system of relations. Such games present a multidimensional model of a multidimensional world and beg to be employed as effective learning tools. When it comes to systems and processes, other learning strategies, whether discussion, direct instruction, reading, or watching videos, do not provide as direct an analogy to the real world they represent.

Figure 1.1 Impact Games' *Peacemaker:* a news report of an event that will increase
tensions between Israelis and Palestinians

Credit: © Impact Games

TALKING POINT: SIMULATION GAMES ARE INTERPRETATIONS, NOT ORACLES; THEY ARE INTERPRETATIONS THAT ENCOURAGE HISTORICAL QUESTIONING

Despite the great power of simulation games in history education, an
essential caveat must be acknowledged, particularly when talking with
others about simulations. Though there are some historical simulation
games designed first and foremost to provide accurate models of the past,
most useful games are designed primarily to entertain or even to persuade.
Historical simulation games, certainly the commercial ones, are vastly
different in their purposes and presentations from, say, interactive physics
models on the computer. This is no problem at all and even offers potential
advantages so long as educators keep two core principles in mind. First is
the understanding that games are interpretations and that part of the very
reason for using them is to help students develop a sense of skepticism,
and practice critiquing these and other forms of interpretations. From this

perspective a completely accurate simulation of the past—something not achievable anyway—would not necessarily be desirable for practicing higher order criticism. Second, the research on discovery learning—which is essentially what using simulations involves—is quite clear on this point: the teacher must play an active role as a guide and resource for inquiry learning to be successful. Part of this active role is encouraging students to criticize the simulations they play. This way, the flaws in simulation games are part of the learning opportunity.

Indeed, treating simulations as interpretations with inherent strengths and weaknesses, leads to another critical benefit these games can bring: the ability to evoke a variety of deep and meaningful historical questions about a topic of study. The ability to pose meaningful questions is one of the skills of the creative thinkers we wish to help develop. The sense a simulation provides of being in the shoes of an actor from the past seems to raise naturally a great number of questions about accuracy and about the options available to actors in the past. It is worth offering an anecdote. In one particular implementation of the game *Rome: Total War*—a simulation of Roman imperialism—in the author's class, 24 9th-grade students were charged to post several detailed blog questions about the real Romans that were raised by the game. Each student then selected one of the questions posed by the class to research and develop into a brief, persuasive, evidence-based essay. The students, without any further prompting or guidance by the instructor, posted an impressive range of deep questions, including:

- How did the Romans treat captured cities?
- What were the strengths and weaknesses of the Roman alliance system in Italy?
- How did distance and geography affect communications between the Senate and armies in the field?
- Did the Romans acquire an empire in self-defense or through active aggression?
- How were sieges conducted?
- What was the role of morale in battlefield victories and how did the Romans raise and maintain morale?

Perhaps most striking, all of these questions have been the subjects of research and writing by professional historians; when presented with a game, these students were able to pose the kinds of questions that experts in the field do.

Would students have raised these questions on their own when faced with text resources or lecture? No solid conclusions in this area can be drawn without formal research. Important considerations suggest, however, that simulation games may inspire deep questions better than texts or lectures. First and foremost, research has demonstrated that students have an unfortunate tendency to accept what they read in texts at face value, especially textbooks. Even the best habitually read to acquire information, unaware that they are actually encountering the author's point-of-view. Without this deep level of awareness when reading, it is difficult to raise challenges and questions about a text. If acceptance at face value is the norm for students when reading texts, is it any more likely that they will readily challenge and question the statements of their teachers if not explicitly asked to do so? Simulation games may well exceed other media in their ability to evoke excellent questions. They provide such a rich experience with a number of opportunities for sidetracks and special cases that there are simply more things happening to students that may provoke questions during the same span of time a text can be read. Second, students may well be more comfortable raising questions in response to a game than they are in response to a text, particularly if their reading of texts tends to focus on establishing facts, rather than engaging interpretations. Again, it will take significant research to explore the role simulations have in provoking historical questions, but there is no reason to suppose they are inferior to texts or lecture in this regard, and good reason to think they may be superior.

TALKING POINT: THE IMPORTANCE OF PROCEDURAL LITERACY

We are becoming more deeply entrenched in a digital world where computer programs provide increasing amounts of assistance, when they are not completely in control, as distributors of supplies, productivity managers, tele-communicators, prognosticators and advisors, and, of course, entertainers. Yet, many do not understand even the basic functioning of computers and computer programs. Theorists on the role of games in learning and popular culture increasingly stress the importance of this procedural literacy, an understanding not of how to actually program a computer necessarily, but of how computers are programmed, how they function, and how they produce the results they do. Procedural literacy requires understanding in some sense the procedures, the algorithms and routines that underlie software. Procedural literacy brings with it several important understandings:

- Games, like more formal simulations used in science, the military, and other realms, have quite precise mathematical models underlying them insofar as all computer code must ultimately be reducible to mathematical/logical propositions and further still to strings of binary numbers. Regardless of how polished, sensible, or impressive the results produced by a simulation, let alone a game, the mathematical models underneath are inherently subject to human bias, ignorance, and error.

• Even beyond the introduction of errors in simulations by programmers and designers, simulations are never as complex as the world they model. Where every variable and its relationship to other variables is identified and quantified in a simulation, the same cannot be said for real-world events where the complete array of factors involved in an event is rarely, if ever, known.

• Therefore though games (and all simulations) contain quantifiable models, those quantifications, being human in origin, can never be perfect. Computer games, computer simulations, in short, computers, are tools not oracles.

These are critical concepts for navigators of today's computer-saturated world. They are derived from a blend of the critical thinking skills humanities-based disciplines like history attempt to cultivate with the more quantifiable logic of the mathematical and scientific. Simulations in the history class provide an outstanding opportunity for increasing students' procedural literacy by serving as quantifiable, dynamic models to critique.

TALKING POINT: USING SIMULATIONS AS A LEARNING TOOL DOES NOT CONFLICT WITH EXERCISES IN CRITICAL READING AND WRITING

This talking point requires particular care, because it relies upon the commitment and follow-through of each individual teacher even more than the other propositions in this chapter. One of the most common immediate objections that comes to mind for those unfamiliar with simulation games is the result of an erroneous equation: learning how to read, write, and argue critically and effectively must decrease when time is given to "playing games," as the most dismissive would view working with simulations. It's as if teachers are required to choose between assigning writing exercises and playing a simulation game; choosing the latter means giving up the former.

In reality, however, this kind of criticism confuses the difference between an instructional strategy involving a particular source material and the critical reading and writing assessments that accompany such lessons. A simulation game exercise is not comparable to a writing assignment, but to a lecture or a movie as a method of instruction available to teachers to help students learn about the past. Students can prepare for and demonstrate their understanding of the historical content and concepts explored in lectures and movies by reading, writing, and speaking. The same is true when the method of instruction is a simulation game. A student can gain experience as an effective analytical writer—word choice, structure, support, argumentation—by analyzing a simulation, lecture, reading, or film—not to mention a variety of other sources of instruction. Simulations, of course, should not replace other forms of instruction wholesale. Effective teachers must choose the instructional strategy or tool that is most effective for the learning outcomes desired. But there is no reason to suppose a student cannot experience an appropriately rigorous course of reading, writing, and discussion when learning from simulation games.

TALKING POINT: THE EFFECTIVENESS OF SIMULATION LEARNING IN OTHER FIELDS

Researchers in math and science education have long been aware that using models is an excellent means of understanding more complex real-world phenomena. Experiments with more controllable physical forces in a lab can help students extrapolate and understand the effects of these forces on planets; tossing a ball can model the trajectory of a cannonball; the list of such practical uses of modeling in education is long indeed. The effectiveness of simulations in these fields is also connected to the practice of using microworlds, digital simulations of a microcosm, to model concepts in science and math ranging from physical forces and chemical interactions to mathematical properties. The elements of a microworld function according to a set of rules, and students can learn how these rules operate by manipulating one component of the microworld and observing the effects on other components. To take a very simple example, one could adjust the temperature in a microworld and observe the effects on a particular gas. By forming and acting on hypotheses, experimenting and observing, students learn about the principles at play in the microworld and, by extension, the physical world. Microworlds have an established record as effective methods of teaching complicated subject matter.

The principle that modeling and simulation are valid methods of learning in science and math can be extended to the study of the past. Since history is a far less quantitative field than science, and simulation games often less precise than scientific models, however, the key is to make sure that the simulations are treated as tools, not absolute truths. This should be the case in science as well, but sometimes at the primary and secondary school level, for convenience's sake, we respond as if the mathematical and experimental grounding of scientific simulations are perfected. Fortunately, the dangers of this sort of reasoning are clearer with historical simulation games; it is far clearer that these games are imperfect models even in the best of circumstances. Nevertheless they provide an initial look at a complex system that can be refined over time. As with microworlds in science and math, when playing simulation games in history, students have access to the "moving parts" of the historical processes in question— the interactions of people with each other and their environment.

THE MISSING TALKING POINT: WHY FUN IS NOT AN ARGUMENT FOR USING SIMULATIONS, AND WHY ENGAGEMENT IS A MORE ACCURATE TERM

The claim will not be made that simulation games should be used in classrooms because they are fun. This is intentional. It is a common mistake to assume that a primary or important reason for using simulation games in the class is because they are fun. This is a misleading, if not wholly inaccurate framing of the issue. Effective lessons can and should intentionally be engaging, but there is a critical difference between engagement and fun.

That simulations offer engaging modern multimedia presentations of the past to today's students is clear. The best simulation games offer radically different presentations of the past from traditional media, combining interactivity, engaging challenges, eye-catching graphics and sounds, and compelling gameplay. These games, both through their accuracies and inaccuracies, can shed light on the past. Games can spark learner interest and engagement, and promote learning through a variety of modes. This point is reasonably self-evident and need only be touched upon briefly. Video games are multimodal, communicating through visual, tactile, and auditory channels. They engage a learner through more than the one or two channels of normal classroom instruction. They do this seamlessly, drawing the learner into a mini-world defined by sights, sounds, visual feedback to kinesthetic controls, and even text. Players make world-changing decisions through these channels.

Make no mistake, when students are engaged in what they are learning, a lesson can be highly effective. Of course, learning in a classroom should never be made unpleasant by design. Nevertheless, fun is simply not a useful concept or a meaningful criterion for selecting and using learning tools. The first problem with the term fun is that it is ill-defined and relative. How is a student supposed to respond if asked, "Was it fun to play, observe, and critique *Climate Challenge*?" Compared to what? Spending time with friends outside school relaxing? Going to an amusement park? Seeing a comedy? Eating ice cream? All of these are fun activities and arguably more fun than being required to critique a simulation rigorously. Even playing the game itself simply for the pleasure it brings is probably higher on the scale of fun than being required to take observation notes, analyze, and assess—indeed you will find in your classes that some avid gamers are dismayed that they have to slow down and analyze, rather than just play a game for fun.

The second and more important problem with the term is that fun is not the equivalent of educationally valuable. We know this. Consider whether you have regularly had teachers who asked the class whether it would be fun to research and write a thesis paper and then cancelled the assignment if students decided the exercise would not be fun. A ludicrous scenario to be sure. Thesis papers are assigned, ideally, because learning to write clearly and persuasively is an important skill and a valid learning goal. Whether the act of researching and writing will be fun is simply beside the point. Continuing along this line, promoting the use of simulation games because they are fun implicitly sets up an unproductive tension between simulation games and other forms of instructional techniques, activities, and assessments, ranging from seminars and lectures, to labs and paper-writing. All can be highly effective educational practices when their strengths are used purposefully to achieved a desired learning goal. This gets obscured when teachers use the term fun as a meaningful criterion for an educational activity.

Finally, it is decidedly not the case that all students will embrace the idea of playing, observing, and critiquing a simulation game. Some certainly will. Others will find the experience intimidating based on how they feel about video games in other contexts. Still others, as strange as it might seem, will feel discomforted by the different approach to learning about the past. This is often the case with the strongest traditional learners. There are a number of students, often the highest performers on traditional assessments, who prefer lecture and recitation because they have mastered getting good grades within this framework. Yet the goals for twenty-first century history education suggest that there needs to be far more to these students' education than simply learning how to receive and give back information and opinions, however sophisticated students may become in doing so. While, everything else being equal, it would be nice for these students to enjoy playing and critiquing simulation games, their enjoyment is not the decisive factor.

Far better terms than fun are engaging, interactive/participatory, and immersive. Lessons that require students to participate actively, to interact with the sources of information, critique them, and construct their own meaning, can be highly effective. Simulation games, employed effectively, can certainly be far more engaging than a typical recitation, worksheet, or lecture, and this is an important reason for their use, when combined with the other points made above.

★ ★ ★ ★ ★

The exact points raised in a conversation about the value of simulation games will, of course, vary depending on the audience and their concerns. Together, however, these points represent some of the strongest reasons available for implementing simulation games in the classroom. Above all, it is important for all teachers, but particularly new teachers, to demonstrate to others that they are purposeful and thoughtful in their decisions to use a simulation game in class. In other words, teachers should be clear that they are selecting simulation games as appropriate learning tools to achieve valuable learning objectives. The following chapters will aid in this purposeful use of simulations, first by exploring in greater detail the qualities of appropriate simulation games.

CHAPTER 2

What Makes a Valid Simulation Game?

Not all games are simulations, and games that are not simulations can be used in a class. A teacher might use a quiz game to motivate students to review, for example, but the quiz game is not in any sense a simulation of the past. Since this book is fundamentally concerned with the unique offerings of simulation games, it will be helpful to survey in this brief chapter the criteria that make some history-themed games appropriate for use as simulations and others not.

WHAT MAKES A HISTORICAL GAME SUITABLE TO USE AS A CLASSROOM SIMULATION?

Even given the definition that a simulation game is a game that models the real world, some debate exists over what the exact criteria for a simulation game are. One could, of course, split hairs. In a sense all games can be said to model the real world, or at the very least some world, to greater or lesser degrees. The question also arises, does the successful modeling of reality make something a simulation or merely the designer's desire to do so? Most teachers, however, need not engage in these debates. Regardless of whether all games can be considered simulations, there are historically themed video games that are not well suited to use as classroom simulations. When selecting games for classroom use, therefore, a teacher must first consider: What makes a particular historically themed game an effective simulation for classroom use?

To determine the effectiveness of a simulation game, remember the primary strengths of the medium. One of the assets of a historical simulation game in an educational setting is its potential to serve as an explanatory model—a system-based explanation of how something in the real world functions. Simulations provide a set of game systems that suggest, through analogy, how systems function in the real world. They offer simplified models of more complex phenomena. As such, they can be a powerful means to explain the constraints and possibilities within which people in the real world lived and acted. Understanding these constraints and possibilities is an important part of understanding why certain historical outcomes were more likely than others.

Unlike a professional flight trainer or medical simulator, however, many of the games considered here were created first and foremost to entertain. By their very nature, then, these game systems will produce varied outcomes based on the vision of the designers, decisions the player makes, the operations performed by the game's artificial intelligence, and the results of any randomness built in. These varied outcomes are a core part of what makes these programs games. A player of *Political Machine*, for example, will win the presidential election in some games, lose in others, but always play a unique game. Because the outcome of a game will change with each play through, and because game designers often readily and regularly concede historical accuracy to appealing gameplay, the primary strength of simulation games is not as static descriptions of some factual details about the past. Text or image is often better suited to illustrating, say, how a specific city looked at one specific moment in time. The strength of the simulation, on the other hand, is to model in more-or-less broad terms how that city functioned. This strength must be taken into account when critiquing simulation games, whether those games are commercially produced for entertainment, or designed by non-profit social activist groups. Inaccuracies in specific details should be noted, but are not the sole means by which an effective simulation should be judged.

Since valid simulation games need not, and indeed cannot, represent each and every historical detail accurately, the criterion for an effective simulation game, instead, is this: *Its core gameplay must offer defensible explanatory models of historical systems.* "Defensible" is the operative word here. In the discipline of history, arguments offered by one historian may be rejected by the next. The propositions that endure become historical convention, the arguments that have held up to criticism due to the strength of their explanatory power and the strength of the supporting evidence. There is always room for a historical convention to be undermined; indeed it is a time-honored tradition in history to challenge conventions. By these standards, then, to be considered a historical simulation, a game must offer an interpretation that is defensible: reasonable based on the available evidence. It also promotes the idea so critical for training flexible, creative thinkers, that when it comes to humans interpreting and making meaning of the past, there are far more shades of gray and maybes than certainties.

The value of using defensibility as a standard is that it encourages students to think about what can and cannot be sustained by historical evidence. So long as a game has enough historical merit that students will be challenged to critique its validity, it is worth consideration for classroom use. Indeed, inaccuracies in the game serve a useful function: they give students an opportunity to challenge, just as the accuracies give them a chance to support.

Let's look at some examples of games with defensible interpretations. *Civilization* offers an excellent example of the distinction between accuracy in the sense of correctly representing the specific details of all events and states from the past and accuracy in the sense of offering some defensible arguments about world history. Any number of particulars in a given round of *Civilization*—the Zulu civilization discovering flight and dominating the player's English civilization, or the Assyrians discovering fusion technology in 1800—could be historically inaccurate. As a general model of how civilizations develop and interact, however, *Civilization* offers some highly defensible explanatory models. Among other things, *Civilization* models the happiness of each city's population and its relation to the productivity of the population. The happiness of a population is determined by a city's size, relative peace, access to food, access to luxuries and entertainment, and access to public buildings that promote happiness (temples, theaters, synagogues, coliseums, churches, etc.). When the number of unhappy citizens outnumbers happy citizens, the productivity of the city begins to drop as some citizens refuse to work in protest of conditions. This drop in productivity does not change until the level of unhappiness is remedied. As a model of governing, this is a very simple one indeed. However, it is a useful and reasonable explanation of why rulers could not devote all their energies to exploiting a populace, building weapons of war, or other one-sided activities. The model indicates—again it must be noted, on a simple scale—a fundamental feature of political power, one especially true of the pre-industrial world: to rule effectively, one must have the consent, if not outright support, of a certain number of the governed.

Above all, *Civilization* suggests that geography, particularly the allocation of natural resources, is a major factor in international conflict, and a major reason why some civilizations in world history have grown to be more militarily and politically powerful than others. The civilizations that have the best land to settle and access to most abundant and varied resources will, if led well, tend to be more powerful than those civilizations that lacked such advantageous geography. That one can seriously argue that the dominance of Europe in nineteenth-century global affairs is based in large part on advantageous geography is clear from Jared Diamond's bestselling work, *Guns, Germs, and Steel* (Diamond, 1997).

Let's consider another example. In *Political Machine* the player manages the U.S. presidential campaign for a Democratic or Republican candidate in a general election. Each turn represents one week of game time and the candidate's available actions each turn are limited by their stamina points. Every action costs a set number of stamina points; when those are exhausted the turn is over. As noted earlier, play centers on sending the candidate to various states to make political speeches and advertisements addressing the concerns of voters in that state. *Political Machine* offers very reasonable portrayals of presidential campaign map strategies, issues concerning voters in 2008, and the statistical profile of voters' political leanings. The game also presents a critical truth of campaigning. A candidate cannot be everywhere and do everything. Instead successful candidates must be selective in the states they frequent and the messages they stress. Furthermore, no serious real-world presidential campaign can succeed without money, and raising and managing funds is critical to a winning strategy. Each turn the candidate can raise funds in a state. Doing so, however, comes at the cost of stamina points that could have been used to publicize the candidate's message. Making trade-offs between fundraising and other political activities is a core issue in the game. Too much time fundraising will prevent the candidate from persuading enough voters to win the election; too little time, and the campaign will grind to a halt, starved for money. These are all defensible explanations.

Less defensible components of the game concern the functioning of political operatives and political endorsements. Both can be acquired by building specialized variants of the campaign headquarters: the outreach center and consultants' office. Each state with an outreach center adds to the candidate's public relations points. These can be used to obtain endorsements from national organizations lobbying for gun rights, civil liberties, environmental stewardship, and so on. Consultants' offices, on the other hand, generate political capital points. These can be used to hire political operatives in a given state. The methods of acquiring these operatives and endorsements are problematic, but there is no question that these are parts of modern political campaigns and the treatment in the game provides a useful spark for a conversation about reality.

The simulation is mostly limited to the extent that it is superficial. The positions that candidates take lack all nuance. Candidates are limited to indicating their support or opposition to an issue and their opponent's stance. With most issues, this is too unsophisticated. In the case of the war in Iraq, for example, indicating support or opposition hits the essential point, perhaps, but leaves out any subtleties. So, for example, the argument made in 2007 that the U.S. should either commit more troops or withdraw from Iraq is lost. High gas prices offer a second example. Some candidates in 2008 focused on concerns about U.S. fuel independence, others focused on global warming, still others on the need to develop alternative fuel sources. In these and many more issues, the details of policy debates are lost, reduced to support or opposition.

This simplicity, however, can be viewed as a caricature of U.S. presidential elections or a legitimate fundamental critique of the campaign process. Consider that the player can potentially win election by visiting key states and simply issuing speeches and ads that tell the people of the state what they want to hear—in other words it is possible to win the game by following the polls rather than crafting a coherent principled platform. It is a regular criticism of presidential campaigns that candidates cannot win by being completely truthful and consistent in their principles. Another related criticism of presidential elections is that candidates that win election do not fulfill all the promises they made while campaigning. Finally, the game suggests that candidates need to move from their respective political wings to the center if they want to win elections. Combine these factors with the critical importance of money to winning an election, and the simulation can be said to offer some defensible interpretations of the pressures involved in a general election and how those pressures can influence candidates.

The distinction between the accuracy of the particulars of *Civilization*, *Political Machine*, or other simulation games and the validity of the general explanatory models in any given session is critical and must be handled with care by educators. Interestingly enough, this distinction parallels to some extent the distinction between history education as rote memorization of pre-established data and conclusions and history as the search for patterns in evidence in order to draw meaningful conclusions about the past that are always subject to challenge and revision. If one sees the core of history as a "learn the established dates, events, facts, and conclusions" approach, video games will have little place in the curriculum. Returning to *Civilization* for a moment, one could easily play as the Zulus, yet build the pyramids and cathedrals, be the first to industrialize on the globe, and conquer the pre-industrial English. Playing *East India Company*, onc could play as the French, yet drive the British from India and secure dominance over the region. These things did not happen in the chronicle of the past. Hence, one might erroneously conclude that games that allow such alternative pasts to be generated have no place in the learning of history. But one might just as easily assert that counterfactual history, competing interpretations, and debate will also have little room in a limited interpretation of history, though all are established components of the discipline.

In point of fact, a simulation cannot actually be a dynamic working model of the past and at the same time reproduce every historical event and detail in ways that match historical conventions. Consider why this is so: a black box that returns an exact match to historical events each time is not a working model; it is a static representation of what happened. This is not to say that a teacher should ignore the inaccuracies of a game. If a student playing *Europa Universalis* somehow manages to create a seventeenth-century Germany politically unified by Hanover it is critical that the student either already be aware or come to learn that, really, Germany did not become a nation-state until the nineteenth century. Here the teacher has a critical role as guide. Certainly, knowledge of the fundamental points of information and evidence is essential to any meaningful historical analysis, and teachers must help guide students to be aware of factual inaccuracies in game interpretations. The work of history, however, moves far beyond that knowledge into problem solving. The past was not predetermined; rather, key factors in the past made some historical outcomes more likely to be successful than others. Understanding the past in terms of environmental factors, social forces, and actors' decisions combining to make a range of possible outcomes is a critical part of historical understanding.

When critiquing simulation games, therefore, a teacher must take care to ensure students know there will be inaccuracies in the historical specifics of a game and help them identify those inaccuracies. The past was not predetermined, however, and if a simulation game is to allow the player choice at all, there must be the possibility that outcomes can be reached that did not occur in the past. The real question when judging a game, however, is how effectively does the game model some of the historical factors that constrained and provided opportunities for people making decisions in the past?

At the other end of the spectrum from games like *Civilization* and *Political Machine*, *East India Company*, and *Europa Universalis*, are games in a historical setting that offer few or no reasonable models of historical systems. To be a valid simulation game, the game's core systems should model specific historical systems, or, to put it another way, the historical elements of the game should be a fundamental part of gameplay. Otherwise, the game is a just a video game whose action happens to be set in a historical period. It offers no defensible explanations for why and how historical events were caused. While there are assuredly valid educational uses for such games as forms of new media and illustrations of cultural beliefs, these games are not the most effective when the purpose is to critique historical models—they are simply too far removed from an actual simulation.

Assassin's Creed provides a clear example of a game that, while set in a richly detailed past world, offers no viable explanations of the past, and is, therefore, not really an effective simulation. Set in a lavishly depicted

Levant in the age of the Crusades, *Assassin's Creed* offers an outstanding snapshot of medieval urban architecture and daily life in the major Crusader cities of Acre, Damascus, and Jerusalem. In the role of Altair, a member of a shadowy but powerful assassins' guild, the player navigates the byways and rooftops of these carefully reconstructed twelfth-century cities in order to assassinate key targets within the local power structures. The buildings exhibit a mix of classical and Islamic architecture, and the key historical sites, such as the Dome of the Rock in Jerusalem, dominate the landscape. The streets teem with the activity a historian might expect from a medieval metropolis: day laborers wander the streets, street preachers harangue the crowds about the impositions of the Latin crusaders, vendors hawk their wares, and everyday people go about their business fetching water, visiting merchants or discussing the day's business with neighbors.

Despite its beauty, richly rendered and reasonably authentic looking environment, and engaging gameplay, however, *Assassin's Creed* is not a simulation game, or, at least, not sufficiently a simulation game to warrant its use by history students. This is not because the game is far too violent—bearing a mature rating from the ESRB—for use in many educational settings. Nor is it because the back story of the game places the player in the highly fictional role of the modern Desmond Miles, who controls his ancestor, Altair, through a sort of time machine/body possessor known as the animus. This latter lack of realism could easily be overlooked if the merits of the game as a simulation in other aspects warranted it.

The fundamental issue that prevents *Assassin's Creed* from serving as a simulation is twofold. The historical accuracies in the game are largely irrelevant to the core systems in the game. On the flip side of the coin, the core systems in the game are not intended to, and do not, provide defensible models of historical systems. Thus the game does not offer serious explanations, even implicitly, about historical cause and effect in the world of the Crusaders. Gameplay centers on Altair's fantastic acrobatic abilities, weapons skills, and stealth techniques. While the settings are provocative and the story makes fair use of the political, social, and religious tensions in the Crusader states of the late twelfth century, the historical aspects are simply a backdrop for the action. They serve as description, rather than model. The player has little, if any, opportunity to be part of any historical systems in the game. Ultimately, any effort to critique the historical accuracy of the game would be reduced to considering factual details—did this character exist, was that building actually in medieval Jerusalem, did street merchants operate in the streets of Damascus?—not analyzing historical systems. Indeed, one could easily conceive of the core gameplay—interrogation, acrobatics, assassinations, and melee fights—taking place in any number of alternate settings, fantastical or otherwise.

None of this diminishes the success of *Assassin's Creed* as what it is: a game. It is thoroughly engaging and exciting, and its designers clearly did not wish it to be a historical simulation. There is nothing wrong with a game simply being a game. When the goal is to teach systems analysis and historical interpretation, however, using valid simulation games yields the best results. Because the core of *Assassin's Creed* is not focused on modeling historical systems, and does not, as a result, offer any meaningful explanation of historical systems, the game is not the most effective for history education.

The examples provided by these various games help establish the following parameters. While an effective simulation will demonstrate reasonable historical models with its core gameplay, teachers and students must take care not to equate the sum presentation of established historical events and facts within a game with the validity of its historical models. Granted, a game like *Assassin's Creed* that deviates so far from the documentary record should be ruled out as a historical simulation. A simulation game useful for learning about the past, on the other hand, while not statically projecting all the details of the past, must offer valid models of reality in its core gameplay.

Even with this criterion of valid models, however, it is still clearly open to debate what games fall within the boundaries of "accurate enough." All simulations have strengths and weaknesses. The key is whether the accuracies are overwhelmed by the inaccuracies to an extent the teacher deems to be unacceptable. As a general rule, however, games that are too simplistic, cursory, or abstract in their representation of systems in the past are probably not good candidates for classroom use. *Rise of Nations*, for example, an older real-time strategy game where players attempt to build their historical civilization and conquer all rivals, is an example of a game that is less suitable for classroom use. There are some historically valid points, but most of these have to do with the styles of architecture and types of military units available to a given culture. The underlying model of the game is problematic. A player must have his workers mine gold, cut wood, and hunt/gather/harvest food from a finite area of land. From these three resources, each of which can be exhausted, all military units, buildings, and civilization advances are built. The civilization that manages to conquer its rivals, generally through superior armies or simply well-timed attacks, wins the game. While, on a certain level, the presentation of history as a madcap materialist struggle to collect enough resources and build enough units to squash one's rivals might ring true to a certain extent, it is, at best, an overly simplistic model and, at worst, quite misleading. The major oversimplification of the fundamental game model outweighs the minor accuracies. None of this detracts from the fun of the game; it just makes it less suitable as a tool for student-historians.

In all of this, the abilities and ages of students and the goals of the lesson play an important role in assessing the appropriateness of a particular game. If the primary goal is to use the game to analyze a set of real-world systems, appropriate at all age levels but particularly for younger students, the game should display reasonably sound models. The more sophisticated the students, the more able they will be to handle oversimplifications with a grain of salt. Furthermore, if the goal of a video game unit is to subject a game to extensive critique using a variety of sources, a game can be more inherently flawed. The flaws serve as fuel for the critique; one can learn just as much about the past by challenging a flawed interpretation as by affirming a sound one. Depending on the ages and abilities of students and the level of critique desired, it will be more or less up to the teacher to provide the structure, resources, and frames of reference to handle a more or less accurate simulation game. Less accurate games, in general, will likely require teachers to provide students with greater scaffolding.

★ ★ ★ ★ ★

Now that we have considered the qualities of an effective simulation game, it is time to survey the main types of historical simulation games available and consider the strengths and weaknesses of each genre in addressing core curricular content in history, geography, and economics. This is the task of the next chapter.

CHAPTER 3

Matching Genres of Historical Simulation Games to History and Social Studies Curricular Content

Now that we have considered the basic criteria for identifying an effective simulation game for the classroom, it is time to consider the various genres of games available and how these genres fare when it comes to addressing common curricular content in history and social studies courses. Commercial historical simulation games, and many free ones, can usefully be thought of as generally belonging to one of seven main genres: city-building, nation-building, trade, political management and tactics, life management, war, and combined nation-building/real-time battle. Games in each category will focus on different periods and places in the past and even different aspects of the category. Still, the common features of each genre generally lend themselves well to lessons about certain kinds of social studies curriculum content, and less well to others. The trade games, *Patrician 3* and *East India Company*, for example focus respectively on fifteenth-century northern European trade and seventeenth- to nineteenth-century European trade with South and Southeast Asia, but both address core issues in economics. Since the core gameplay and content of a successful simulation game implementation must meet the curricular demands of a course, this chapter surveys the general connections between particular social studies curricular concepts and the various genres of video games.

In the United States, social studies curricular concepts, especially in public schools, are heavily influenced by state academic standards. These, in turn are ideally derived from or at least consistent with the voluntary standards established by national academic and professional bodies such as the National Council for Social Studies. The existence of standards in and of themselves is not problematic; working together as individuals and institutions to develop meaningful educational goals for social studies and history is a worthy goal. The problem, however, is that states increasingly assess whether students are meeting the academic standards by administering standardized high-stakes tests that may not accurately measure real thinking ability within a discipline. Regardless of whether this changes any time in the near future, it seems certain that national bodies will continue to offer explicit sets of academic standards and reasonable to suppose that states will also continue to do so. Therefore, it is reasonable to approach social studies content through established content standards. This book will not survey individual U.S. state standards, however, for several reasons: not all states have drafted formal content standards for the social studies; those who teach in private schools are often less constrained by state academic content standards; and readers outside of the United States will have obligations to their own particular curricula. Instead this chapter's consideration of social studies content is based on the more common ground of the voluntary standards promoted by the following U.S. national standards-setting organizations:

- The National Center for History in the Schools (National Standards for History)
- The National Council for Geographic Education and the Association of American Geographers (National Geography Standards)
- The Council for Economic Education (National Economic Standards).

The guidelines from these three bodies are at the core of a number of curriculum standards in social studies shared by various states in the U.S. and across international borders. So, readers can be confident that their use of progressive and effective game-based pedagogies can, as needed, be made wholly consistent with demands of "the standards." Readers not bound by these particular standards should have no difficulty recognizing the core concepts from history, geography, and economics education identified in them throughout this chapter.

THE GENERAL STRENGTHS AND WEAKNESSES OF SIMULATION GAMES

Like any medium representing the past, simulation games have a blend of strengths and weaknesses. There are certain elements of human culture, society, and history that simulation games, by their very nature, are particularly well suited to model. When designed well, these games do an excellent job illustrating the cumulative effects of decisions over time.

Whether it's the production of resources in a city, the growth of trade networks, the impact of a flanking maneuver on an enemy unit's morale, the success of a protest, or the importance of advertising in a political campaign, simulations illustrate how decisions made early on can have dramatic impacts over time. Closely related to the modeling of decisions is the modeling of how different factors influence a system over time. Whether the factor is the geographic position of a city, the funds available for a campaign, or the constraints of poverty, simulations illustrate how constraints can shape development of individuals, families, businesses, peoples, and nations over time. Perhaps best of all, the replayability of simulations allows players to explore the impact of different decisions over time by changing their choices each gameplay session.

Simulations also do a superior job allowing students to explore the impact of finite resources in human societies. One of the defining characteristics of much of world history, especially for pre-industrial societies, is scarcity, the simple reality that for most people, most of the time, resources have been severely limited, as have the abilities to produce, transport, and communicate. Even in the modern world, most people, institutions, and nations generally find themselves in situations where their resources are finite, if not greatly limited. Playing most simulation games requires the player to experience working with finite resources and in conditions of scarcity directly, albeit virtually, whether in the form of a civilization's research capacity, a city's finances for energy reform, or a campaign's war chest, and to decide how to allocate limited resources to achieve goals.

This limitation on resources is a fundamental part of the modeling of trade-offs, the hallmark strength of simulation games. Games, for the most part, are about choices, and historical simulation games tend to focus on making choices under a set of limitations. As noted above, the most obvious limitation in most simulation games is the scarcity of resources. But trade-offs are also the result of the simple reality that one cannot be everywhere and do everything at once. The player of a presidential campaign simulation can only target one state at a time, and the tension between fundraising or delivering the campaign message is always present. The player of a life management game can only send a family member to be trained for one job at a time. In simulation games, as in life, every time the player chooses to devote resources to something, or to take a particular course of action, they also, consciously or not, choose not to do something else. Most decisions that are subject to historical analysis involve trade-offs where there is no clearly better answer, just a question of goals; simulations are highly effective at immersing players in these kinds of situations.

Where simulations do not fare as well are in modeling situations where it is difficult to establish a set of quantifiable variables and relationships.

Most of all, simulation games, at least single-player ones, are not currently particularly good at modeling complex interactions between individuals. Large scale social dynamics are one thing; they can be modeled using quantifiable variables. Sophisticated negotiations, diplomacy, really conversation of any sophisticated type, however, are beyond the capabilities of most computer games. When the goal is to model human conversations, roleplays and board game simulations still tend to be more effective, though it should be noted that there are multiplayer games that blend the strengths of computers to quantify and model with the power of human negotiation.

A BRIEF SIDE TRIP: TURN-BASED GAMES, REAL-TIME STRATEGY GAMES, AND SCRIPTED DECISION-MAKING GAMES

All computer games can be divided into turn-based and real-time games depending on the way time passes in-game. Though the subject matter and style of play can vary greatly, turn-based games tend to have core set of features. Like the classic board games of *Monopoly*, *Sorry*, and *Candyland*, play is divided into turns, and each player has the opportunity to complete one or more actions during a turn. Once those available actions are exhausted, the player ends their turn, usually by clicking a button. In single-player, turn-based games the player often competes against one or more computer-controlled opponents that take their turns after the player. So, for example, in *Civilization* games the player makes the moves for his civilization, ends his turn, and waits for the computer artificial intelligence to make the moves for each of the rival civilizations in the game. In multiplayer turn-based games, each human player takes a turn in sequence. Other turn-based games pit the player against an environment rather than a specific opponent. In these games the player takes her actions, ends the turn, and receives some form of report or feedback about the impact of her actions, as calculated by the game. This is the case in games like *Ayiti*, where the player determines whether each member of her in-game family will seek employment, enroll in school, or recuperate for the season. When the turn is ended, the game provides an end-of-season report indicating the results of the player's choices. Turn-based games divide play into breaks and pauses; since turns are generally untimed, students have time to survey a situation and take time to plan their actions before executing them. This makes such games good candidates for including sophisticated strategic elements and providing complex options for action.

A special variant of turn-based game found primarily in small web-based simulations is the scripted decision-making game. Gameplay is reminiscent of *Choose-Your-Own-Adventure*® books of the 1980s, where the reader adopted the identity of the book's main character and turned to different pages depending on the choices made. So too, in a scripted decision-making simulation, the player is presented with a starting scenario often through descriptive text and one or more accompanying images, occasionally supplemented by more sophisticated interactive help. The player must decide how to address the scenario by clicking one of two or more available actions with the mouse. At the most basic level, the actions are defined by text descriptions, like a multiple choice test; sometimes the choices involve clicking on a graphic. After the player makes a choice, a new text and/or graphic description appears narrating the results of the player's choice, presenting a new dilemma, and asking for a new choice.

This is best understood through an example. The BBC is currently home to the largest collection of scripted decision-making historical simulation games. In *Who Wants to Be a Cotton Millionaire* the player is presented with a description of the growing textile industry and then charged with successfully establishing an English textile business. On the next screen the player sees an outline map with Cumbria and Lancashire marked. Clicking on either region causes a text description to appear explaining the potential advantages and disadvantages of the location for building a new cotton mill. After the player decides to build in one of these two locations by clicking on the appropriate button, the next screen appears telling the player whether their choice was a good one and either adding removing from stacks of coins representing the player's profits. Then the player clicks a button to move to the next dilemma, who to employ in the factory. The game continues in this fashion until all four decisions have been made; at the end a summary screen tells the player how well they did. Scripted decision-making games can have a variety of different aesthetics. Some are very text heavy; others rely mostly on images; some have links to help sections and additional reading. Structurally, they are all very similar insofar as they present a set of fixed situations and two or more fixed responses to each situation.

It is too easy to dismiss scripted decision-making simulations as too unsophisticated for high school students. Certainly, they are simplistic in that the scenarios and decisions are limited by their organization to a simple branching structure. They also often use graphical styles, especially those of the BBC, that appear geared for too young an audience. Good scripted decision-making simulations, however, offer a few excellent advantages that justify their inclusion in classroom simulations. First, because they are scripted and they are generally designed to educate, the level of accurate historical information is usually very good, generally enough to provide a brief introduction to a topic and get the player thinking about that particular historical context. *Who Wants to Be a Cotton Millionaire*, for all its simplicity and somewhat playful graphics, does advance an implicit argument: the sole goal for early nineteenth-century factory owners was profit—an argument that held true for many but not all, and an argument certainly worthy of classroom discussion. Second, they are playable in web browsers and, therefore, accessible to everyone with a graphical web browser—the vast majority of computer users today. Finally, they are very short. *Who Wants to Be a Cotton Millionaire* can be played through more than once in 15 minutes by thoughtful players. They can be quite effective, then, as quick introductions to an aspect of the past to foster conversation and provoke questioning.

Unlike in turn-based games, the action in real-time games takes place continuously without division into turns. As with turn-based games, the player may compete against human or computer-controlled opponents, or against the environment. Unless the game is intentionally paused, the timer is always ticking. Consequently, the player makes decisions and takes actions at the same time that opponents act and the environment responds. The battlefield segments of the *Total War* series, for example, take place in real time. The player's troops, divided into units, are semi-autonomous. Left without specific instructions to the contrary, they will fight when engaged by an enemy unit and even chase routed enemies. Because gameplay takes place in real time, the opponent's units are executing commands, maneuvering, moving, and fighting at the same time as those of the player. Real-time games need not be focused on warfare. Games like *SimCity*, and *Dawn of Discovery*, in which players must build and manage cities, require players to balance income and expenditure, manage crises, and supply the needs of the city as the urban inhabitants work, consume food, search for entertainment, and sleep; the clock keeps ticking. Real-time strategy emphasizes decision-making under pressure and an effort to model effectively the times, distances, and spaces involved in executing actions in addition to modeling the acquisition and expenditure of resources in real time.

GENRES OF HISTORICAL SIMULATION GAMES

City-builders

Description

Games in the city-building genre generally operate in real time and focus on the creation and management of one individual settlement of people, whether that settlement is a Roman city, medieval manor, European colony, or modern metropolis. Players attempt to achieve one or more goals, generally expressed in terms of achieving a certain score, earning a certain level of profit, or constructing certain types of buildings. Players must achieve these goals while satisfying the needs and wants of the inhabitants to avoid a failing city. These needs and wants, in turn, range from food and shelter to security and entertainment.

For most city-builders core gameplay generally involves selecting the types and locations of buildings that will be constructed. Some games, however, such as *SimCity*, require players to establish building zones— residential, industrial, and commercial—in which the buildings appear, rather than the buildings themselves. Either way all construction takes place on a plot of land, usually rendered in an isometric view, with various geographic features. Buildings fulfill economic, political, residential, security, and entertainment functions, among others. City-builders often share the mechanic that certain types of buildings work in conjunction with others to meet the various needs of urban inhabitants. Some games require buildings to be connected in what is commonly called a daisy chain. In a daisy chain, a necessary task is completed by a set of buildings, each of which performs one part of the task. In the medieval manor simulation *Stronghold 2*, for example, wheat is grown on a farm, ground into flour by a miller, and baked into bread by a baker (Figure 3.1).

Figure 3.1 A bakery daisy chain in Firefly's *Stronghold 2*
Credit: © Firefly Studios

Other city-builders, such as *City Life*, avoid the daisy chain model, requiring the player only to build a grocery store, for example, to feed nearby inhabitants. However the needs of the city are addressed, most city-builders emphasize that adequate services must be spread sufficiently throughout the city and within reach of residential areas.

Meeting the wants and needs of the population is a common theme in city-builders. These games emphasize forethought in the initial placement of buildings and an ability to respond to a series of changing and growing citizen demands over time, and in real time. Most of all, these games emphasize the balancing act that is effective management. Building more industries than can be staffed by employees or producing less food than needed by the population can result in the collapse of the city economy. Focusing solely on basic necessities leaves citizens without sufficient entertainment to be happy; focusing solely on entertainment leads to a starving populace. Resources are finite and choices must be made how to spend them. Deciding which trade-offs will lead to the prosperity of the city is the player's main task.

Some city-builders focus on modeling social relations and applying social philosophies in addition to planning and managing urban spaces. *SimCity Societies* exemplifies this, allowing players to construct buildings that facilitate a variety of socio-political philosophies and world views ranging from creativity to industry and authoritarianism. *City Life*, on the other hand, requires the player to balance the needs and wants of different social groups that can be tense around one another: elites, suits, the radical chic, blue collars, the fringe, and the have nots, as the game terms these groups.

Curricular Content Addressed by City-builders

Individual city-builders address a number of common history concepts. A fair number of past and modern settings have been treated in this genre. The most recent of these are:

- *CivCity: Rome*, *Caesar*, and the *Glory of the Roman Empire* series focus on Roman cities.
- *Children of the Nile* takes ancient Egypt as its focus.
- *Stronghold 2* addresses the challenges of managing a medieval manor and castle.
- *Dawn of Discovery* focuses on building a late medieval city.
- *AD 1701* examines European settlements in the New World.
- *Tropico 3* is based in a Cold War era dictatorship in the developing world.
- *SimCity* and *City Life* portray modern cities.

Because this genre puts the player in the role of a powerful city manager, it tends to do a good job raising questions about the role of the government in social and economic development and the role of urban settlements in various societies. To the extent that a number of city-builders, notably *CivCity: Rome, Caesar,* and *Children of the Nile* operate within the context of large scale historical empires, they address fundamental issues about imperial administration, including revenue, commerce, civic and private spaces, and many others. Finally, the city-builders do a good job illustrating the fundamental aspects of culture, particularly urban culture, within a given society.

City-builders are also particularly well suited to address common geography concepts concerning the physical environment of a locale. Players are constrained in the layout of their cities by the physical geography. Depending on the particular game, uneven ground, marshland, mountains, and forests can all prohibit the construction of buildings and roads. Cities and settlements, therefore must adapt to the terrain. In city-builder scenarios with limited resources available, players must also make choices about what to build. In *Stronghold 2*, for example, a player cannot construct stone towers without access to stone. If he is playing in a region without any, he must either secure a supply elsewhere, purchase stone through the market; or choose to defend his settlement with weaker wooden fortifications.

Physical geography constrains players, but players also modify their environments considerably in the city-building games, and the impact of humans on the environment is another core curricular concept. Forests are cleared, farms are planted, and buildings and roads are constructed, all permanently changing the natural environment. Indeed the city-builders tend to follow the typically human, and especially Western, assumption that the natural environment exists primarily to benefit humankind. This is particularly clear in *AD 1701*, where the goal of the digital settlers, as it was for many European countries, is to profit off of the perceived inexhaustible resources of the new worlds. It is an interesting point to consider that in gameplay, as in much of human history, there seems to be very little concern about the impact of the humans on the environment and the sustainability of human exploitation of the environment.

The city-builder genre is particularly well suited to addressing certain economic concepts. In these games, the player takes the role of city-designer and manager, constructing a city from the ground up and making the command decisions that lead to prosperity or failure. Operating in conditions of scarcity is a hallmark of these games. The inherent challenge is choosing how to use limited resources to achieve major goals. In some city-builders, such as *Stronghold 2*, the populace harvests resources in the form of stone, wood, and food among others. The player decides how to allocate these resources to satisfy the needs of the populace and the political, military, social, and economic goals of the players. *CivCity: Rome*, on the other hand, uses, somewhat anachronistically, the mechanism of money. Regardless of the mechanism, devoting resources to one area necessitates scaling back in other areas—a core economic concept. Many city-builders also offer an interesting and subtle point of access to the discussion of the government's role in an economy. To a greater or lesser extent, city-builder economies are command economies. The player as the *de facto* head of the government determines to a large extent what resources are acquired and how they will be distributed. This is a concession to game-play: a simulation where individual inhabitants freely operated in a market economy would be more accurate in some scenarios, but would relegate the player to a passive observer—and these are meant to be commercially successful games after all. The drawbacks of command economies are not particularly well illustrated insofar as there is no real alternative in the game, but this is an area that can be explored in class discussion.

Civilization/Nation-building Games

Description

Civilization/nation-building (hereafter called simply nation-building for convenience's sake) games come in both turn-based and real-time varieties. All share a common focus on developing a culture, civilization, or nation through a period of time that can range from a decade to millennia. The player manages the economy, domestic politics, construction, scientific research, foreign policy, military, trade, and other aspects of their civilization, kingdom, or nation. At the same time they struggle with rival states managed by the computer AI. These games call for both skilled micromanagement and insightful high level strategy from players.

The *Civilization* series is one of the major subsets of the nation-building genre. *Civilization III and IV* (Figure 3.2) are among the most used commercial simulation games in schools, and *Civilization V* was released in 2010. There is also a free open source clone of *Civilization I*, called *FreeCiv*. The premise of the series is that the player functions as the guiding hand for a civilization developing from its late Neolithic founding to the early third millennium CE. The computer controls a number of rival developing civilizations. Play begins in the year 4000 BCE on a stylized topographical map of the real world or an imaginary one divided into squares—though the designers of *Civilization V* have opted to use hexagons instead of squares. Cities are the core of a civilization. Their populations

Figure 3.2 The world map in *Civilization IV*
Credit: © Firaxis Games

extract resources from the surrounding land and generate wealth, culture (a quantifiable element in the game), and scientific research. City populations also construct military, scientific, economic, and cultural buildings that enhance the capabilities of the civilization, and construct units ranging from settlers, to military forces, to transports and traders. One of the keys to success in the game is to found and cultivate a large number of cities in advantageous geographic locations. Determining the most effective combination of resources to extract from the areas surrounding the city and converting these into products of civilization is another key element of gameplay (Figure 3.3). Each city's population is represented by one or more workers (each worker = several thousand people). Each worker can exploit the resources in a limited number of squares surrounding the city. Each square can produce one or more core generic resources depending on its terrain:

- bread—generic food to support the population of the city;
- shields—generic raw materials used to construct buildings and units;
- coins—income from precious trade resources or trade routes such as roads and railroads.

Worker and engineer units can also build improvements on a square such as irrigation, roads, and mines. Each of these increases the resource production of the square. The hallmarks of the *Civilization* series are the

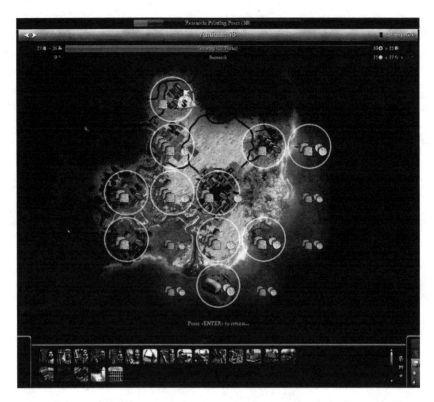

Figure 3.3 A city map in Firaxis' *Civilization IV* showing natural resources surrounding the city. Circles indicate tiles where the city is currently harvesting resources.

Credit: © Firaxis Games

ability to cause and witness grand simulated historical events and engage in complex political, economic, diplomatic, and military strategies. The turn-based format organizes complex sets of decisions and information into manageable chunks and gives players time to reflect and plan carefully before each move.

The second major subset of the nation-building genre is the family of real-time grand strategy games developed by Paradox Entertainment. To note a few examples: *Crusader Kings* deals with the high Middle Ages in Europe. *Victoria II* covers the Age of Imperialism. *Hearts of Iron III* treats the political and military conflicts surrounding the Second World War (Figure 3.4). *Europa Universalis* (currently in its third version) (Figure 3.5) covers nation-building from the mid-fifteenth century to the end of the eighteenth century. All of these games share common characteristics and a similar interface. Victory or defeat is generally determined by a points system, which factors the player's success in developing the various aspects of her nation. Play takes place in real time: the other nations (controlled by the computer) continue to act as the player is making decisions. The default speed is quite slow, however, with one day passing every several seconds. This effectively gives the player a hybrid of turn-based and real-time play: the world, by default, is constantly in motion but can be paused, speeded up, or slowed down as desired. The player manages their kingdom or nation through a variety of actions, including appointing and removing government advisors and generals; moving armies; managing budgets and

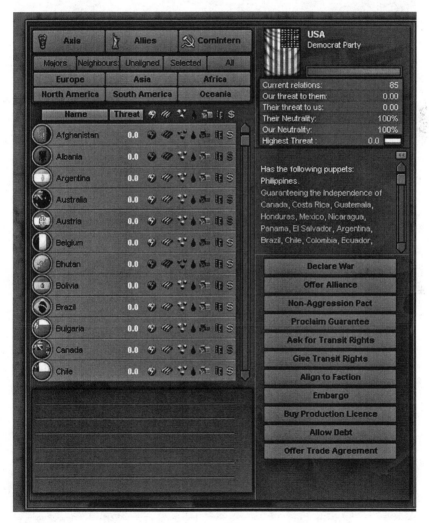

Figure 3.4 The diplomacy screen in Paradox Games' *Hearts of Iron III*

Credit: © Paradox Interactive

Figure 3.5 The world map/strategic map in Paradox Games' *Europa Universalis*
Credit: © Paradox Interactive

trade; and conducting diplomacy. Most kingdom- or nation-wide management decisions, such as adjusting budgets, and making diplomatic overtures,
are conducted through a series of dialog boxes with sliders and various
other controls. Provincial management and military operations, on the
other hand, are conducted on the main map screen, a map of the portions
of the world relevant to the particular game, divided into regions.

Players select specific regions under their control on this map to
produce units and make adjustments to building programs, taxation, and
other aspects of provincial management. They also conduct grand scale
military campaigns by ordering units to attack enemy regions. These games
offer the most comprehensive nation-building simulations available and
are remarkably thorough in their treatment of economic, political,
diplomatic, and military facets. This comes with a relatively high degree
of complexity, however, and these games can be daunting at first to learn.
If time is not too limited, however, they are well worth the effort.

Curricular Content Addressed by Civilization/ Nation-building Games

Though there are many common social studies concepts addressed by most
nation-building games, there are enough distinctions between *Civilization* and
other games in the genre to warrant considering aspects of the former separately.

The *Civilization* series, as has been noted, is not particularly well suited to retracing the exact path of a specific historical civilization. Nevertheless, the game contains a great deal of accessible historical content. The civilopedia, in particular, is a rich resource, providing text and image overviews of hundreds of different scientific, military, cultural, and economic developments from the past. The arcs of scientific and cultural discovery in the game usefully illustrate the corresponding development of past civilizations in broad terms. Researching a code of laws, for example, requires the previous discovery of writing. The tree structure of research, where the current research opportunities available depends on what has already been discovered, does a good job illustrating the real process of scientific and technological developments. The ability to trade advancements and technologies with others also illustrates well the importance of such cross-cultural exchanges to the scientific advances of civilizations. In short when it comes to exploring the main arcs of technological, cultural, military, economic, and scientific developments and their impact on civilizations, the game holds up well to scrutiny. Other nation-building games often have less detailed models of scientific and technological development but offer many avenues for consideration of these issues. Nation-building games in general, most effectively address the history concepts that deal with the growth of nations and interactions between nations. They also address the administration of empire and the economic development of civilizations.

In terms of geography concepts, the *Civilization* series portrays world history as fundamentally driven by the relationship between humans and their environment. From the founding of the initial city, a player extracts resources from the surrounding environment and uses these to produce military, cultural, political, and scientific achievements. The extraction of resources is improved by modifying the landscape: irrigation improves food production, mines allow for extraction of more minerals, and roads and railroads increase trade. In the later stages of most rounds of *Civilization*, the landscape is largely transformed by human activities. Cities dot the map, each connected by a network of roads and surrounded by high intensity farming and mining operations. There are limits to the exploitation of the land, however. Human activity generates waste and pollution and, left unchecked, this pollution damages the environment. There is also a limit to how much land a city can exploit. Interestingly, though, the resources produced by a square are infinite. So long as the square is not modified or shut down by pollution, it will continue to produce resources at a consistent rate throughout the game.

Civilization also highlights the role of geography in regional conflicts. Each civilization has a cultural and political boundary that expands with the cultural influence of the civilization. When a military unit violates the boundaries of another civilization, diplomatic friction and even outright wars can be sparked. Conflicts over access to resources are also common with powerful civilizations attempting to bully weaker ones into trading valuable strategic resources such as iron, coal, oil, and uranium.

Nation-building games other than *Civilization* tend to focus more on political geography than physical geography. Regions have unique topographies, but these games generally omit considerations of specific natural resources. To the extent that friction between regions is common in these games and there are a variety of reasons for such conflicts, these games also examine the geographic concepts of cooperation and conflict. Furthermore, the Paradox-style games that operate in real time do an excellent job portraying how slowly armies and navies moved in the pre-industrial and even industrial world.

Civilization and other nation-building games revolve around the economic problems of allocating resources most effectively in conditions of scarcity. Success in these games requires a balance of scientific, economic, and military development, all of which require the construction and main-tenance of effective infrastructures. Devoting too many resources to one aspect can leave the player falling behind in others. The economic concept of growth is also usually an important part of these games. Players must decide how to invest resources based on the payoffs they expect in the future. Researching new weapons can lead to a more effective military; construct-ing trade routes can lead to a higher national income. The role of trade in enriching nations and civilizations is also integral to most nation-building games. Finally, it is worth noting that though nation-building games tend to simulate the strengths and weaknesses of representative government better than the city-builders, they still essentially model command economies because of the player's overarching control of most economic decisions.

Trade Games

Description

Trade is an important component of city-builder and nation-building games, but trade itself in these games is mostly conducted in the background by the computer as a line item in a budget. The handful of games com-prising the trade genre, however, place the player directly into the role of a merchant who must purchase, transport, and sell goods. Most of these games focus on the pre-industrial world: *Port Royale* on the Caribbean of the seventeenth century, *Patrician* with late medieval and early modern Northern Europe, and *East India Company* with the Euro-Asian trade in

Figure 3.6 The port information screen in Nitro Games' *East India Company*
Credit: © Nitro Games Ltd.

exotic goods (Figure 3.6). These three entries in the genre focus on maritime trade, though some much older games, notably *Merchant Prince*, include trade by land, and there is an entire wing of trade games like *Sid Meier's Railroads* that deal with the topic. It is reasonable to suppose future land-based trade games will be developed.

In each of these games the player begins as a merchant with a starting sum of money and a small fleet, often one ship, in a port city that is part of a trade network. Each city in the network has a marketplace where the player can purchase and sell trade goods that vary depending on the period and place depicted by the game. The player purchases a cargo, directs her ship to another trade city and sells the cargo. If the player follows the fundamental economic principles of buying low and selling high, or at least selling items for more than they cost to buy, her wealth will increase. This allows players to hire more ships, purchase more goods and, in many cases, start to develop their home port city by increasing the size of warehouses, for example, and upgrading the shipyard to produce more sophisticated ships.

Curricular Standards Addressed by Trade Games

Trade games tend to address very specific history and geography concepts: the role of trade in the development of a particular civilization/nation, for example, and the idea that regions can be defined by trade characteristics; some can be used to address considerations of the geographic concept of movement in the form of goods. Not surprisingly, these games shine when it comes to addressing economic concepts associated with trade. Beyond the very concept of trade itself and its role in distributing resources across and between societies, a number of other economic concepts are addressed. The modeling of finite resources is in full effect, and players must choose how to spend their limited money on trade goods, fleets, and port upgrades. The idea of marginal costs and benefits is also at work as players decide which shipments balance risks and rewards, costs and payoffs. Similarly the idea of growth is a key factor, that investments in certain areas—larger warehouses, for example—cost resources now but can lead to increases in profits later. Finally, many of these games employ models of prices that fluctuate based on supply and demand, which makes for a realistic but challenging element as the player must be ready to find prices in a port for the goods he is transporting have changed since the last time he visited the city.

Political Management and Tactics Games

Description

Though similar in some respects to nation-building simulations, political management and tactic games are a broad group that focus either on seeking or maintaining political power in a modern democratic/parliamentary state or challenging the existing regime. They share an attention to political tactics, particularly tactics designed to influence the attitudes of various constituencies, There are three subgenres, one that focuses on elections and electoral strategy, and one that focuses on governing, and a third niche category that focuses on resisting oppressive regimes.

Political Machine is an excellent example of the electoral model. As noted in the previous chapter, this simulation requires players to manage a presidential campaign by sending their candidate to various states to make political speeches and advertisements addressing the concerns of voters. While the candidate initially has access to the top three issues of concern in a state, more become available if a campaign headquarters is constructed there. The candidate makes speeches and ads to publicize her stance on a particular issue or that of her opponent. Voters in the state may be swayed depending upon their political leanings and the type of media used for the advertisement. Fundraising, seeking political endorsements, and employing political operatives round out the strategic options in the game. Some electoral games focus on more specific features than a general election. USC-Annenberg's online serious game, *The Redistricting Game*, for example, explores how changing congressional voting districts in a fictional state produces very different voting patterns. Players try their hand at both partisan and bi-partisan gerrymandering scenarios in addition to an attempt to ensure that voting minorities are represented. These and other electoral games vary in their gameplay but share a common theme of focusing the player on issues of voting and voter opinion.

Other games, such as *Commander in Chief* and *Democracy*, assume that the player has won election to the presidency or prime ministry and must now deal with the problems of the country. Actions in these games generally take the form of increasing and decreasing levels of funding for different programs and initiatives and adjusting policies in areas ranging from taxes and the economy, to defense and education, just to name a few. In addition to the effect these decisions have on the country overall, different political groups and constituencies will react positively or negatively to the player's political decisions, resulting in greater or lesser political support. The voting public's approval is critical for the player to remain in office.

Finally the games *Freedom Fighter '56* and *A Force More Powerful* focus on resisting a regime. The former puts players in the roles of young Hungarians participating in the revolution of 1956 through taking part in demonstrations and a variety of resistance activities. The latter is a larger scale model of non-violent protests. In AFMP players can engage in a variety of scenarios representing real-world issues. All revolve around using non-violent protest tactics against a regime to influence political change.

Curricular Standards Addressed by Political Management Games

Political management and tactic games tend to be quite modern in focus; they are at their best addressing representative democracies and parliamentary states of the past few decades and conflicts with twentieth- and twenty-first-century regimes. The accuracy of any particular game in modeling the organs of government will be mixed; when a game allows one to be the head of a generic democratic state, there will certainly be problems of over-generalization. These games excel, however, in raising issues about political trade-offs in the modern state. Whether on the campaign trail, in office, or demonstrating on the streets, there is neither enough time nor resources to achieve everything, and players must decide which goals they will pursue, goals that, as in the real world, will please some constituencies and anger others. Consequently, political management games are a good choice for government and civics classes, in addition to classes and units focused on recent political history and current events.

To the extent that they incorporate financial and other economic activity, political management simulations address a number of economic standards. These games, like most every other, model the economic problems of allocating resources most effectively in conditions of scarcity. In this case the primary issue is how to allocate limited funds to different policies and programs. The particular economics concentration, however, is on the relationship between government and economy in the form of taxation and business regulation.

Life Management Games

Description

Life management games share the central premise of putting players in someone else's shoes—usually someone less fortunate—and challenging them to survive and thrive. They are intended to build empathy and understanding, an appreciation of the problems that billions of humans face daily. The commercial serious game, *Real Lives* (Figure 3.7), is the most comprehensive of these. The player is randomly assigned a newborn character in a family from virtually any nation on the globe. Gameplay is of the turn-based, player-versus-environment variety. Every time the player clicks the "age a year" button, his character ages and a series of events affect him and his family. These are determined through statistical considerations: so a family in Bangladesh has a higher likelihood to suffer through floods, and certain African countries are far more likely to experience civil war. Events can also be personal, ranging from succumbing to diseases, gaining and losing jobs, and suffering from political oppression. These events affect the health, happiness, and wealth of family members, all of which is presented in a series of tables and graphs. A journal feature records these critical events in the player character's life, providing a narrative overview of gameplay. Until the player's character is old enough to make simple decisions, he must simply passively experience fortune and misfortune. Once the character is old enough to make decisions about school, life, relationships, etc., the player selects different priorities from turn to turn and watches as those priorities influence the character's life.

Free, online, life management simulations tend to focus on one specific place and lifestyle rather than the wide scope of *Real Lives*. *Third World Farmer*, for example (Figure 3.8), is a provocative and engaging game designed to illustrate the extreme hardships of modern subsistence farming in a developing nation. Ultimately, the player, as the decision-maker for a farming family, decides which crops to plant and livestock to raise while staying within a tiny budget. If the player's family acquires more wealth,

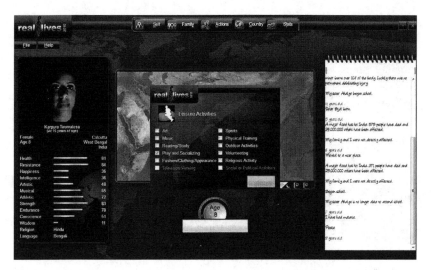

Figure 3.7 The main screen of Educational Simulations' *Real Lives*
Credit: © Educational Simulations

she can raise more expensive livestock, build simple farm improvements, and even bribe political representatives so that her family's farm is not harassed by corrupt government officials. The player must also monitor the health of her family and can send one or more family members to gain an education. Health care and education, however, are not free, and, as with everything else in the game, the player must decide how to satisfy disparate needs with an income that is always too small. *Ayiti*, on the other hand, illustrates the problems associated with poverty for a family in Haiti. The player still manages a small family. Instead of choosing between different crops to grow, the choices are about jobs, household spending, and education. One cannot get the best jobs without an education, but school costs money and keeps one from contributing to the family income. Some of the best paying unskilled jobs, like working in a rum distillery, take a toll on the health of a family member working them, making them more vulnerable to injury and sickness. There never seems to be enough time and money to achieve anything more than a basic subsistence.

Curricular Standards Addressed by Life Management Games

Though the settings vary, most life management games address the struggle of living with too few resources. All a player's efforts to improve their family's standard of living can be wiped out by drought, disease, or even

Figure 3.8 Selecting corn, wheat, and cotton crops in *Third World Farmer*
Credit: © Third World Farmer Team

marauding forces in a civil war. Most runs through these kinds of game, the player will find themselves frustrated by how little progress they make. In presenting some of the difficulties of life in a developing nation, they address a number of different curricular concepts. In terms of history, these games offer a glimpse at diverse societies but are often firmly rooted in the historical issues of decolonization, the Cold War, and contemporary global issues. The geographic standards best addressed by these games are those concerning the general relationship between humans and their environment, and issues of political geography. These games do not tend, however, to delve deeply into the precise relationships between humans and the terrain they inhabit. Life management games excel, unsurprisingly, in addressing economic issues. The trade-offs required when there is a scarcity of resources is the clear overarching theme. Growth is another critical issue in many of these games. Players must decide how to invest their meager resources, though unlike the more optimistic city-builders, the payoff for those investments often does not come to pass. Finally these games illustrate how difficult it can be to subsist in so many countries.

Strategic and Tactical War Games (Turn-based and Real-time)

Description

One of the oldest genres of simulation games, turn-based war games are, to a greater or lesser extent, adaptations of the board games of Avalon Hill and other companies that flourished from the 1960s to the early 1980s. Turn-based war games pit the player, as commander of an army, against a human or computer-controlled army. Typically, armies are represented by unit markers on a political or topographical map. Depending on the scale of the scenario, a unit marker can represent a squad or a whole army, and the style of unit markers ranges from groups of figures reminiscent of those found in miniature figurine war gaming to chits labeled with standard NATO military symbols.

Each unit has a certain distance it can move in a turn, generally expressed as a number of movement points. Games that focus on tactics and smaller strategy often illustrate unit movement on maps divided into hexagons (hexes). Games that focus more on large scale grand strategy divide the map into irregularly shaped provinces representing different geographic regions. Other games dispense with map divisions altogether and, instead, calculate allowed movement more organically by considering the distance of the planned march and the terrain traversed. In some games the player moves units and attacks enemy units all within a turn, and then the opponent does the same. Games that strive for a higher degree of accuracy allow both the player and computer opponent to issue orders, and then carry out those orders simultaneously; this latter method allows units to exchange fire and forces players to give orders with less-than-complete information available. So one can, for example, order a unit to take a position that is unoccupied only to find that the enemy has also dispatched a unit to the same position, in which case a skirmish will result.

Depending on the scale of the game and the format of the map, the player may be able to engage in some small unit tactics. In games where each unit represents only a few hundred men and the map is divided into hexagonal spaces, it is possible to encircle enemies and make flank attacks. In games where the armies are large and movement occurs between regions, the player simply sends their forces into battle. The computer then calculates the outcome without any consideration of the placement or facing of individual units. Either way, the outcome of combat is determined by calculation. When combat is initiated the game determines the outcome using formulas that incorporate the characteristics of each unit involved. Units generally have at least one number, a combat rating, which indicates their general strengths. In more complicated games units may have attack and defense ratings that vary depending on the type of enemy unit encountered—infantry, for example, is generally more effective against other infantry units than against tanks.

Depending on the scenario in question, players may try to take and hold critical locations, destroy a certain number of enemy units, or keep at least one unit of their army in play for a certain amount of time. As other turn-based strategy games do for their subjects, turn-based war games slow down the frenetic chaos of a real battle and give the player time to consider moves carefully. What these games may lack in terms of a realistic portrayal of the actual conditions of battle they tend to make up in their accurate portrayal of battlefield maps, historical units, and the relative strengths of each force.

Unlike their turn-based war counterparts, real-time war games allow the human and computer players—or other human opponents—to give orders to their units as quickly as they can and wish, and units begin executing commands as soon as they are received. It takes time for units to execute most orders as they rearrange, march, or prepare to attack. Units operate semi-autonomously, fighting when engaged and even chasing defeated enemies unless previously given a standing order not to do so. Unit operations also are affected by distance and terrain: though the player can quickly order a unit to attack an enemy across the battlefield, the unit will need time to travel and engage, doing so while the battle develops around it.

The real-time battle components of the *Total War* games currently offer the best real-time battle simulators in the field. In these games the player-commander controls units with the mouse, ordering them to change their formation, wheel and about-face, run and walk, and attack and retreat. Each unit has an attack and defense strength in addition to a morale value. When a unit's morale dips below the breaking point, it will be routed and flee the battlefield. Otherwise a unit will continue to fight unless destroyed or ordered to disengage. The battle continues until one army has completely fled the battlefield or, less often, been completely destroyed.

The advantage of these real-time battles is that, unlike their turn-based counterparts, they can give a more realistic depiction of how actual military units conducted themselves in the field. The individuals in a unit of line infantry in *Empire: Total War*, for example, fire in rows, and then reload their muskets. When maneuvering, individuals shuffle over the terrain and have to realign to maintain proper formation. Since the individuals in a unit are represented, some can be in the rear lines spared from direct fighting while the front lines are actively engaged. Perhaps most importantly, the number of autonomous units and the real-time setting can create very chaotic battlefields. The most orderly pre-battle plans ultimately degrade in the chaos, and successful commanders have to adapt quickly to changing conditions. Elements such as these create a level of realism not readily matched by turn-based war games.

Curricular Content Addressed by War Games

These are niche games where the study of the past is concerned. In cases where battle or war itself is integral to a unit or course, war games offer the potential for superior insight, especially as a companion to eyewitness battlefield accounts. So *Medieval II: Total War* allows students to participate virtually in the campaigns of the conquistadors against the Aztecs, and *American Civil War* allows students to shoulder the burdens of commanding the Army of the Potomac. These simulations illustrate to a greater or lesser extent the costs and challenges of war and the historical factors that led to defeat or victory. The real-time battles of the *Total War* series also offer a particular advantage over typical methods of instruction about war. They allow students to consider at closer range the so-called "face of battle," the nature of warfare from the perspective of individual soldiers. Rather than presenting wars as a series of dated battles and outcomes, they can be used to provoke students to consider the human element of battle.

Hybrid Nation-building/War Games

Description

Rome: Total War (RTW), *Medieval 2: Total War (MTW)*, *Empire: Total War (ETW)*, and *Napoleon: Total War (NTW)* are the most recent creations in a series of strategic and tactical war games by Creative Assembly—*Shogun 2: Total War* will arrive soon to offer an updated simulation of feudal Japan. Currently, the *Total War* series is the standard for combining turn-based nation-building and grand strategy with real-time tactical battles. Understanding the basics of the *Total War* series allows one to shift quite readily to other turn-based/real-time hybrid military games. The turn-based campaigning simulates the political, military, economic, and diplomatic expansion of the Roman empire, a medieval kingdom, a rising eighteenth-century nation, France under Napoleon, or Japan in the period of warring shoguns, respectively. The real-time battles simulate the troops and tactics of these different periods and places. In *RTW*'s campaign mode, the player controls a faction, representing one of the great Roman families. As ruler of a Roman faction, the player has a starting town in Italy as a power base; as a faction leader, she is given missions by the Senate, which she can complete or ignore. Over time it becomes increasingly likely that the player will be pronounced a renegade by the Senate. At that point she may attempt to take Rome itself and become its ruler or continue on as an independent ruler of an empire. Players may also opt to be rulers of other Mediterranean powers, instead of the head of a Roman faction, and struggle against Rome for control of the known world. The open ended campaign ends when the player has conquered a certain number of territories. Subsequent *Total War* games follow the main conventions of *RTW*. In *MTW* family factions are now rival kingdoms and principalities in Europe and North Africa. Missions are supplied by councils of vassals and the pope. *ETW*, in turn, places the player in the role of absolute monarch of a European nation, with the option to be a ruler in Asia or Africa. Missions in *ETW* are no longer assigned; it is up to the player as monarch to determine her objectives. *Napoleon: Total War*, functions very similarly to *ETW* but with a campaign mode that assigns tasked based on the historical campaigns of Napoleon. *Shogun: Total War 2* will likely follow the same template as its predecessors, but place the player in command of one of the warring factions of feudal Japan.

Two important elements of the nation-building campaign mode in *Total War* games are city/province management and army management. Each city (or city and province in *MTW*, *ETW*, and *NTW*) produces a sum of tax income based on the current tax rate in the city, the city's population, and the types of buildings it has. If the player controls a city, she can construct improvements there. These range from roads to places of worship and markets. Improvements affect the happiness of inhabitants, the wealth generated by the city, and the kinds of troops that can be levied there. Each city, so long as it possesses the required buildings and funds, can also recruit various kinds of soldiers each turn. Players are constrained in their choices of building construction and unit recruitment by two primary factors. Each city can only construct one building and recruit one military unit at a time; many buildings and military units require more than one turn to complete or levy. Second, each city improvement and unit requires a certain sum of money to build and maintain. Therefore the player must balance income and expenditure if she wishes to maintain a strong empire. *ETW* and *NTW* extend this model by making the province the center of development, not the city. Buildings and improvements can be placed throughout the province, and these increase the abilities of the main city in the province to generate revenue and recruit troops.

The other main elements of the campaign mode are strategic movement and diplomacy. A military unit produced by a city can become the core of a new army or join an existing army of one or more units. Armies can be led by faction leaders, generals, or obscure officers. Each army is represented by a single figure on a stylized physical map of the game world. There are no squares or hexes, however; each army can move a finite distance on the maps each turn depending on the terrain along the route and the types of units in the army. The player also controls diplomats. Diplomatic actions between the player and other powers can include trade arrangements, truces, alliances, ultimata, and wars. Either the player or a computer-run faction can initiate battle between armies or an army and a fortified settlement. Battles are tactical affairs carried out in real-time. The type of terrain where opposing armies meet on the strategic-level campaign map dictates the dominant terrain on the battlefield: hills, woods, coastline, desert, mountains, etc. Battles can also take place around villages and cities or consist of outright assaults, in which case the relevant fortified structures are included.

Curricular Content Addressed by Hybrid Nation-building/Real-time War Games

The *Total War* series provides details on the politics, military, religious practices, culture, and architecture of various periods and places. In addition, each simulation offers plausible models for the creation, administration, and maintenance of empires, core elements in national history standards. *Empire: Total War*, moreover, offers insights into the rise of Western military dominance over the globe. The *Total War* series, as many nation-building games do, suggests that the expansion of human cultures and governments is aided by certain geographic features (plains, rivers) and hindered by others. Allocation of scarce resources is also a key component of *Total War* style games. Player-commanders must choose which kinds of troops to recruit, where to place armies, and where to build defenses, with only limited resources to commit. The economic concept of growth is important in these games as players decide how to invest resources in the present to secure future payoffs. Essentially, *Total War* style games combine a reasonably easy but sophisticated nation-building component with an integrated treatment of warfare in the context of nation-building.

THE PROBLEMS AND PROMISE OF FIRST PERSON GAMES

First person games, or "first person shooters" (FPS) as they are generally known, represent an important category of historical strategy games that, nevertheless, will not be examined in this book. It is important to understand what this genre is, however, and how games in the genre tend to operate. Many of the principles of FPS games have great potential to be harnessed to the needs of serious historical simulations, though most currently do not do so.

The principle behind FPS games is that gameplay is presented in first person perspective. In other words, the player sees a representation of what their character would see in the game. So, the player's character is not seen onscreen beyond perhaps his hands and the tip of a weapon, if one is used. To see different parts of the world, the player must operate controls to turn their avatar's head and eyes or move their body. This sort of format allows for a high level of immersion; the player can feel like they are in the world they see on the screen.

Though the first person experience genre offers the potential to develop all types of gripping historical simulations and some experiments have been made in this area, the vast majority of first person games involve some form of ranged weapon combat, hence the standard name, first person shooter. By far, most historical FPS games focus on World War II. In these games, the player takes the role of a soldier, most often an infantry soldier, and engages in a series of firefights as part of a campaign. These games tend to focus on fast paced, intense episodes packed with highly stylized, graphically violent, cinematic style combat. Eventually, the genre may develop to include games that are not focused exclusively on combat. For now, however, the genre tends to be highly violent and rated for mature audiences. Most pointedly, these games require the successful player to point simulated real-world weapons at simulated real-world humans and shoot, a feature that makes them patently unsuitable for most formal educational settings, certainly in middle and secondary school.

POSTSCRIPT: SERIOUS GAMES AND CONTEMPORARY ISSUES

Though most commercial games can reasonably be categorized according to the genres introduced in this chapter, there are many commercial and even more non-profit simulations that do not conform so easily and offer different treatments of historical and contemporary issues. An increasing number of games of this sort have been designed recently to educate and inform, with entertainment as only a secondary goal. These so-called serious games tend to be narrower in scope. At times, though certainly not always, these games can contain higher levels of accuracy than commercial games. Serious games tend to be designed by smaller production teams that are interested in teaching the general gaming populace about a particular subject. They tend to focus on contemporary issues and, accordingly, provide an excellent complement to the offerings of commercial simulation games. Recent commercial serious games (at the time of writing) include:

- *Global Conflicts: Palestine*: report on conflicts in Palestine and Israel as a journalist.

- *Peacemaker*: serve as the Israeli prime minister or Palestinian president and negotiate a lasting peace.
- *Real Worlds 2010*: live the life of an individual anywhere on the globe. Make key decisions about employment, education, political and leisure activities and guide the fate of your avatar.

In addition to these commercial products, there are a number of free serious games available. These are usually web-based games that run in the player's Internet browser, like *Third World Farmer*. Some other examples include:

- *Ayiti*: make economic decisions for an impoverished family in Haiti, hoping the family will survive and, ideally, increase its standard of living.
- *Climate Challenge*: act as a powerful president of the EU charged to reduce the emissions of greenhouse gases in the EU and secure global cooperation with greenhouse gas reduction. The player must achieve these goals while maintaining a strong economy and keeping the voting population content.
- *Against All Odds*: flee an oppressive Eastern European home and seek sanctuary in a new country.
- *Energyville*: determine how to supply the energy needs for the city of the future.
- *Stop Disasters*: Protect a city from disasters like floods and tsunamis through construction of preventative and protective measures.

See Appendix A for a complete list. The serious games movement is young but has a promising future. Small, independent developers will likely continue to develop small focused games that engage without sacrificing interpretive power and defensible models. Of course, flaws in interpretation and differences of opinion can always be found, no matter how well-intentioned the game; these serious games should be approached as interpretations, as texts not scriptures, just like the commercial games. In the final analysis, they offer treatment of a far wider variety of topics than the commercial games and, accordingly, are very useful.

CHAPTER 4

Instructional Strategies

Once the curricular concepts and learning goals for a simulation exercise have been determined and the appropriate hardware and software have been arranged, it is time to develop a lesson plan by considering the instructional strategies that will be used to introduce students to the simulation and provide the necessary structure for them to study, analyze, and reflect on it. More specifically, teachers must consider:

- the methods students will use to play and analyze games;
- the opportunities for reflection, analysis, and discussion that will be provided;
- the types of historical resources to provide students and the timing for introducing them;
- the products students can create to demonstrate their learning.

The next chapter will survey a variety of activities, exercises, and projects that can both enhance and serve to assess student learning. Now, it is time to examine the core instructional strategies that should be part of any game-based learning environment.

When planning instructional strategies, the idea of a teacher as a designer of learning tools and environments is a powerful concept to adopt from the field of educational research. For practical purposes reflective, purposeful, and self-improving classroom teachers already are educational designers. They develop learning tools and environments in an iterative process. First, they consider the needs of their students as learners, gleaning useful knowledge from educational research, and working with core learning objectives in mind. Keeping these considerations sharply in focus, they design resources, tools, and environments intended to achieve the desired learning goals. In response to the real-time information gained while implementing a lesson in the class, the environment, tools, and resources are modified to address more effectively the needs of the learners and the learning objectives. These revisions are put into practice and refined further in response to more classroom implementations; and so the cycle continues.

This lens of design is well suited to an approach where simulation games are used as learning tools. A computer game, as a complex interactive multimedia tool, by its very nature becomes a central piece of any learning environment of which it is a part. It fosters experimental, hands-on learning. By itself, however, a simulation game is not a sufficient learning tool. Rather, successful game-based lessons are the product of well-designed environments. Teacher/designers must thoughtfully embed these games in an environment and set of learning activities where students, learning tools, and resources work together in pursuit of the desired outcomes. Lessons are revised, shifted, contracted, and amended in light of classroom practices in an iterative and reflective process involving teacher and student. In other words, game-based learning environments should begin with a sound design that is then adapted to the needs of the learners. It is in this spirit that the chapter explores the key elements of designing a lesson based on a simulation game.

INTRODUCING STUDENTS TO A SIMULATION SESSION

Talking About Simulation Games

Before jumping into the study of the simulation itself, prepare students to adopt a critical stance by offering some introductory comments to the class. There are two core sets of ideas at work that may require explanation. The first is that of system, process, and contexts. The second is of simulation games as models of systems and processes, and providers of context. The critical points distilled here from earlier chapters are:

Historians, social scientists, and scientists, among others, are primarily concerned with understanding systems and processes. This is a concern with how things work together and how certain causes produce certain effects.

Games are made up of systems and processes. Simulation games model real-world systems and processes and do so in dynamic, complex fashions.

Playing within a system, such as a simulation, is a superior way to understand a system. The models in good simulation games tend to offer reasonable analogies to real-world elements. This is why governments, businesses, and the military, among others, have their people play simulations as a part of their training.

It can be helpful during this process to ask students for examples of systems (the circulatory system, rain cycle, legislative system, and the cafeteria system, to name just a few examples). It is also helpful to ask students to diagram the parts of a system after providing a sample diagram. Depending on where students are in their understanding, they may never have thought of history and the social sciences this way, in which case, additional care must be taken to adjust their conventional ideas.

For lessons that will explicitly include an element of criticism, some introduction to the idea that history is an interpretation is appropriate. Ideally these concepts have been introduced to students on prior occasions. If not, the teacher should include some of the following ideas that have been raised in earlier chapters:

History is not the past. Where the past is everything that happened before now, history is the active interpretation and reconstruction of the past based on valid sources of evidence.

The most important tasks of the historian are to interpret and reconstruct elements of the past in meaningful ways and critique the validity of others' interpretations.

The ability to critique others' interpretations of the real world is critical for educated human beings. We all encounter multiple interpretations of the world daily. Schools, governments, religious and political leaders, celebrities, and the media offer versions of reality that are often in conflict.

Critiquing the accuracy of simulation games, which present interpretations of the past and present, is an excellent way to develop skills of historical criticism.

Finally, it is a good idea to reinforce that the point of game-based exercises is not to learn passively from the game, but to play an active role in applying the game's models to the world and judging the value of the game as one plays. The primary questions are, "Is this what it was/is like?" and "If this is accurate, what conclusions can I draw about the past?"

Content Pre-tests

Before playing the simulation game it can be helpful for students to orient to the relevant historical content by taking a formative pre-test—one that is used to guide the lesson rather than serve as a grade for students. This serves several purposes. First, it directs students to the types of issues they will consider in the game. Second, it provides the teacher with a sense of what students do and do not know about a subject before playing the simulation. This information can help when deciding which topics need more focus and which less. Finally, a pre-test can be taken again at the end of the unit as a means to assess the learning that took place during the simulation lesson or unit.

Ideally, a pre-test should include a range of questions addressing knowledge and comprehension, analysis, interpretation, and evaluation, perhaps even opinion. A wide range of questions can give greater insight into what students know, think, and feel about issues. The following example from the *Political Machine* contains such a variety of questions.

Box 4.1 SAMPLE PRE-TEST FOR *POLITICAL MACHINE*

Pre-simulation Questionnaire

On a separate sheet of paper or on the back of this one, please answer the following questions using complete sentences.

1   What do the following terms mean?

Red state:
Blue state:
Electoral votes:

2   How does one get elected to be President of the United States?
3   What do you think the most important factors are (not should be, but are) in determining whether a candidate is elected president?
4   If you were a Democratic candidate for president, on which of these four states would you spend the most campaign resources and why?

California, Texas, Oregon, South Carolina

5   If you were a Republican candidate for president, on which of these four states would you spend the most campaign resources and why?

California, Texas, Oregon, South Carolina

6   What is the role of technology (any technology, not just computers) in presidential elections?
7a   How important is money for running a successful presidential campaign?
7b   How much money is needed to run a successful presidential campaign?
7c   What is money used for when running a successful presidential campaign?
8   One common criticism of elected presidents is that they do not fulfill all the promises they made while campaigning (in other words, things they said they would do as president, they did not do). If it is true that presidents do not fulfill all their electoral promises, why don't they?

STRUCTURING QUICK LESSONS FOR SHORT GAMES

Many web-based games designed to educate, persuade, and inform can be easily played in 20 minutes or less, particularly scripted decision-making games. The more free-flowing turn-based player vs. environment games take a bit longer but still can be played usefully in less than 1 hour. While, fundamentally, the organization of lessons using these sorts of games is based on the same principles of play, observation, analysis, and reflection, it is helpful to consider them as a separate category in terms of practical implementations.

Several common features of short web-based simulations distinguish them from their longer, larger counterparts. They often can easily be learned with no formal instruction. These games are designed, usually, for a general audience with little specialized gaming skill. The scripted decision-making games are the extreme when it comes to ease of use. More sophisticated games like *Ayiti* and *Climate Challenge* require a bit more effort to learn to play but are still generally much less difficult than the average commercial computer strategy game. Since play revolves around using the mouse to interact with fixed graphical objects, these games are also generally easy to learn and require at most, a few instructions from the teacher. Instructing students to ask one another for assistance playing works very well for these sorts of games. Those who apprehend the requirements of gameplay more quickly can help their classmates in need. In practice, this means that games of this sort can be given to students without planning elaborate formal training, and total playing time can be limited to anywhere from 20 to 60 minutes, depending on the game.

This ease of play makes note-taking an easier task. The number of decision points in most scripted decision-making games is small, generally somewhere between four and eight total. In practice this means students can note scenarios and options presented to them, their choices and the reasoning behind them, and the results of those choices. Boxes 4.2 and 4.3 provide a generic worksheet for taking notes on any scripted decision-making game and a specific example.

Scripted decision-making games are generally highly focused in their subject matter and the interpretations they offer. This focus is both a strength and a weakness. If the goal is to explore in detail a variety of open-ended options and the interactions over time between sets of variables (food supplies and happiness, access to resources and profits, etc.), these games are too limited. If the goal, on the other hand is to engage an interpretation of a specific historical character's options and the potential result of those choices in a limited set of circumstances, scripted decision-makers are an excellent choice. A focused observation sheet goes a long way to helping students learn about the content in these simulations and some potentially valid interpretations of the past.

Other short web-based games, generally speaking, present students with more decisions and details than scripted decision-making simulations. Observation sheets, accordingly, should have space for students to include these extra details. The great variety of player-versus-environment games makes it extremely difficult to present a generic form for a note-taking sheet. While the particulars of each game may differ greatly, however, the core features to note in any of these games are similar:

- the player's role and goals;
- the scenario or scenarios in which the player finds themselves;
- the resources available;

Box 4.2 OBSERVATION SHEET FORMAT FOR A SHORT SCRIPTED DECISION-MAKING SIMULATION

Simulation Observation Sheet

Title:

Take notes on the following aspects of the game. Paraphrase or quote relevant game text and describe graphic features to illustrate and elaborate upon the points in your notes.

I. Simulation Introduction:

- Player's role:
- Player's goal:
- Types of decisions the player will have to make:

II. First Decision

- Situation:
- Available options (include advantages and disadvantages of each option):
- The option you chose and your reasons for doing so:
- The result of the choice (*include how the game presents the result, and whether it was positive or negative*):

III. Second Decision

(repeat topics from First Decision)
[etc.]

Box 4.3 HYPOTHETICAL COMPLETED SHEET FOR
WHO WANTS TO BE A COTTON MILLIONAIRE

Simulation Observation Sheet

Title: Who Wants to Be a Cotton Millionaire? (BBC)
Take notes on the following aspects of the game. Paraphrase or quote relevant game text and describe graphic features to illustrate and elaborate upon the points in your notes.

I. Simulation Introduction:

Player's role:
  "You are an advisor to a budding businessmen in Kendal."
Player's goal:
  Help the businessman make decisions that will lead to financial success.
  The businessman is surrounded by a stack of money.
Types of decisions the player will have to make:
  Decisions are for a textile business' (1) location, (2) workers, (3) power, and (4) investments.

II. First Decision

Situation:
  Choose where to locate the business. Map with two areas given.
Available options:
  Cumbria ‡ "fast flowing streams" + skilled textile workers; and Lancashire ‡ "fast flowing streams, coalmines and a skilled workforce but it means relocating."
The option you chose and your reasons for doing so:
  Cumbria: can use the streams to power a waterwheel for the factory, workers available there, no need to relocate so I save money.
The result of the choice (*include how the game presents the result, and whether it was positive or negative*):
  Cumbria has "poor communications."
  Textile workers know wool, not cotton.
  Neither of these points was brought up in the description of Cumbria when I made the choice.
  The conclusion the game gives ‡ "A bold choice perhaps!"
  Lose two stacks of money.
  Seems negative—I lost money—the stacks disappear from around the businessman.
  (*etc.*)

- the choices the player can make, the choices the player does make, and the reasons for those choices;
- the results of the player's choices.

In addition to these topics, teachers may also want to include terms and special content contained in the simulation. This is especially the case if special terms will be part of later discussions and assessments. Since one of the goals for observation sheets, in all seriousness, is to train students to be observant, some prompt should be included for students to describe how the game conveys information: the art style, sound, text, and other components. Boxes 4.4 and 4.5 offer sample sheets for the Global Kids simulation, *Ayiti* and the BBC simulation, *Trench Warfare*.

Box 4.4 HYPOTHETICAL COMPLETED OBSERVATION SHEET—*AYITI*

Simulation Observation Sheet

Title: Ayiti: The Cost of Life
Take notes on the following aspects of the game. Paraphrase or quote relevant game text and describe graphic features to illustrate and elaborate upon the points in your notes.

General Information (Get your information from the starting screen about the Guinard family and the next screen "Help")
Describe the starting scenario. Be sure to include a description of the player's:

    Role/Character:
    Goals:
    Challenges/Obstacles:
How is time divided up in the game?

Year 1, Rainy Season

Situation

Family size and status of family members

Diplomas and goud

Living conditions

Jobs available (note best and worst paying job)

Decisions—include an explanation for each decision you made

Belongings purchased

Jobs taken

Changes in living conditions

    Did anything happen to individual family members during the season? If so what?

    What events happened during the season and what effect did they have on your family?

    What were the results of your choices for the season?

Year 1, Summer Season

[etc.]

Whether in the course of completing observation sheets or as a separate assignment, students should be asked to draw some tentative conclusions about the game's interpretation based on their observations. In other words, they should consider what the game designers suggest about the topic portrayed. Otherwise they have missed an important point that the simulation is a historical source, not a neutral record.

STRUCTURED APPROACHES FOR WHOLE CLASS GAME SESSIONS

Class Observes a Demonstration of the Simulation

As noted before there are times when a very effective lesson can be developed where only one copy of the simulation is running and projected for the whole class to see. This can be done as a solution to hardware or software limitations, but it is also an effective pedagogy when the game in question will require more time to master than is warranted for the learning opportunities provided. When the goal is to use a complex game to illustrate a system in action briefly, present a few key concepts, or provide

Box 4.5 HYPOTHETICAL COMPLETED OBSERVATION SHEET—*TRENCH WARFARE*

Simulation Observation Sheet

Title: Trench Warfare

Take notes on the following aspects of the game. Paraphrase or quote relevant game text and describe graphic features to illustrate and elaborate upon the points in your notes.

General

Describe the starting scenario. Be sure to include a description of the player's:

- Role/Character:
- Goals:
- Challenges/Obstacles:

Mission 1

Describe the scenario for the first battle:

List the three weapons you selected for the first mission. Describe each and indicate why you selected them.

Weapon	Description	Justification
1		
2		
3		

Describe how the game depicted the battle. Include a description of sights, sounds, color, and text.

What conclusions can you draw from the outcome of the battle? Consider whether you were attacking or defending, the weather, and the weapons you used.

Mission 2

[etc.]

a target for limited historical criticism exercises, having the teacher control the game allows students to focus on the simulation itself, not on issues of controlling it.

In these cases teachers should prepare students for the exercise by discussing simulation games and, if desired, by assigning relevant reading on the topic ahead of time. On the day when the simulation is to be used, the teacher controls the game while students take observation notes. As with all cases where observation notes are being taken, students should be provided with guidelines for the sorts of things in-game they should note. The teacher may solely direct the course of the play session or may solicit input from students about what course to follow. Either way, it is most effective to pause play regularly and ask students questions in order to monitor their comprehension and challenge them to engage in critical thinking.

Class Plays One Instance of the Simulation Together

This is similar to the demonstration approach in that students do not directly control the game. The important difference is that students make gameplay decisions that the instructor or an assistant implements. Students still take observation notes, and play is paused regularly for discussion. Now, however, each major action in the game is the result of class discussion. This approach combines the advantage of needing only one computer (and a projector) and the advantage that students need not spend time on learning gameplay while still engaging students to interact with the simulation world.

There are several ways to implement this sort of learning activity depending on the size and dynamics of the class and whether the game is single player or multiplayer. These are presented in Box 4.6.

Regardless of how the class is organized, the key to this instructional strategy is that students can engage with the game more directly, interpreting the feedback from the game, making decisions, and issuing instructions to be carried out by the game controller. Single player games of all varieties can be played this way. The most effective games are those where the number of options in a turn is fairly limited or can be articulated simply. With proper preparation, this could be said of many games. Life management games, for example, which tend to have a more restricted range of options, are an excellent candidate for this type of play. Most, if not all, web-based serious games also fit the bill. Other simulations may take a bit more planning, but can be adapted to whole-class play. So, for example with:

Box 4.6 SOME OPTIONS FOR ORGANIZING A CLASS TO PLAY ONE INSTANCE OF A GAME

I. Options for a Single Player Game

A. If students are not assigned to groups:

- Class discusses what to do each turn; final decision made by teacher or through class vote

or

- A randomly selected individual decides what to do each turn

B. If students are assigned to groups:

- Each group discusses strategy for next game round. Then:
- One group is selected randomly to offer instructions for the next game round

or

- All groups present their instructions; the set of instructions to follow that turn is selected by the teacher or through class vote

II. Options for a Two Player Game

A. Students are separated into two teams (each team acts as one player, controlling one side in the game):

- Each team discusses what to do each turn. The team comes to a decision by voting, consensus, random selection, etc. according to the age and interpersonal dynamics of the group.

B. Students are assigned to multiple groups. Half of the groups represent one side in the game. The other half represents the other.

- Each group for a side discusses strategy for the next game round. Then:
- One group on the side is selected randomly to offer instructions for the next game round

or

- All groups present their instructions; groups on that side vote on set of instructions to follow that turn

City-builders: students create a basic plan and build order for the initial core buildings of the city.

Trade games: students issue general orders for starting and ending ports, goods to purchase and sell. Another possibility for a trade game with multiple fleets is to have each team in charge of a different fleet and in control of a percentage of the overall funds available.

Again, the key to adapting games for whole-class play is to reduce the number of options for the class so that they can make meaningful decisions without being overwhelmed by the finer details of gameplay, which they will not have had time to experience and learn.

STRUCTURING GAMEPLAY FOR GROUPS AND INDIVIDUALS

In a carefully designed learning environment, gameplay itself needs to be structured thoughtfully. This can make the difference between a focused learning experience and a wasted opportunity. The main factors in designing a successful set of gameplay sessions are:

- training students to play the game before requiring them to conduct an analysis;
- forming effective play teams;
- reinforcing observation skills;
- fostering reflection.

Generally speaking, a standard structure can be used for productive classroom gameplay by groups and individuals. Students need to learn to play, gain solid play experience, observe and analyze the game in action, and have time to reflect and debrief.

Teaching Students to Play

Any well designed lesson centered on gameplay must factor in the time and instructional strategies required to train students to play the simulation. This point cannot be overemphasized. For games of any complexity— essentially all commercial strategy games—deliberate plans must be made to train students before asking them to analyze. Simple browser-based games can be learned fairly quickly by following the in-game instructions. In a simulation of any greater complexity, however, the teacher needs to provide strategies for students to succeed, particularly if time is an issue.

This point is well worth stressing. Perhaps the most common mistake made when implementing these kinds of lessons is to assume students will quickly learn how to play even a complex game without explicit training. Despite some exaggerated reports to the contrary, the 10–25 age group is not innately gifted with the ability to play computer games. Though relative to previous generations, these students have a tendency to be far more technologically savvy, some simply are not that comfortable with computers and some do not play video games. PCs equipped to play current video games can be quite expensive, and a number of students who consider themselves "gamers" tend to play action games on less expensive consoles, such as Xbox 360®, Playstation 3®, and Wii®. Console gamers often have little experience with historical strategy games, which tend to run on PCs. Those who are accustomed to fast-twitch arcade style games, which reward the ability to read a screen and respond as quickly as possible, will find the complexity and challenge of an average PC strategy game demand a significantly greater amount of reflection and thoughtfulness to play. Even those who are comfortable with playing web-based computer games through social networks like *Facebook* will find the challenge in commercial strategy games significantly greater.

All of these students can learn to play historical simulation games. No doubt if they were sufficiently motivated, as hobbyists are, they could learn the game by themselves. In the classroom setting, however, students generally need to be taught to play. In short: *students need to learn how to play the simulation game to the point that they can understand the models contained within, and it is the teacher's responsibility to provide the resources and support for them to do so.*

Several caveats apply here. First, while students should be expected to learn to play, they should not strictly be assessed based on their ability to win the game. Winning or losing is secondary—one can learn just as much about a game's model of the world through losing as through winning. Announcing to students at the beginning that their goal is to know how to play and understand the game, not win the game, can allay stress for those who feel they are "no good at video games." In addition, it is important that students are clear not to confuse the strategy games they will play with their distant cousins, the fast-twitch arcade type games. A high degree of manual dexterity will never hurt a game player, but is not necessary for success in most strategy games, especially turn-based ones. Communicating this point can also help allay some students' concerns.

Second, learning to play a game is a real opportunity to get students, particularly strong traditional learners, outside of their comfort zones. Games reward experimentation and mitigate risks through the ability to save games and replay scenarios. When students are tasked in groups to immerse themselves in a world and figure out how to operate, they are being given an important opportunity to develop their skills of collaboration and problem solving. This kind of learning experience, though not formally tied to any particular discipline, should not be underestimated. It is often an alien experience for many students, who have come to equate taking risks with courting failure. The trick for the teacher is to build students' self-reliance and willingness to take risks by providing effective support. For example, students can be trained to play in class, provided with a pointed summary of game strategies and techniques, and then assigned to play the game and simply experiment and learn. Add a formal requirement that they play for at least 1 hour, if not more, and have their saved game to show the progress they made. Explicitly encourage students to take risks. Assure them they cannot break the game and need to learn through trial and error. Another effective strategy for promoting self-reliance, or at least reliance on resources other than the teacher, is to have students use a forum to ask each other questions about gameplay.

The teacher is responsible for providing the resources and environment for students to learn basic gameplay and must take steps to make sure students do, in fact, learn to play. It is not necessary for the teachers to be experts in the games they use, but they should be familiar with playing the game. There are several effective options for training students to play a game. The majority of commercial games—including demo versions— have good tutorials that allow players to learn the game's mechanics as they play. It is critical to the financial success of complex commercial games to engage players quickly and fully so that they will want to learn how to play. Successful commercial games, therefore, tend to have effective training mechanisms, and these can be harnessed for classroom purposes. In some cases it works very well simply to allow students to play the tutorial as many times as needed before progressing to the demo game or the full commercial game. Identifying experts within the class, students that grasp the game quickly, can further facilitate the training process. These experts can help their classmates with the game. Doing so increases the collaborative value of the lesson. It also gives experienced gamers in the class the satisfaction of being an expert at something related to class, a taste of success. Not least of all, it keeps the class running at a reasonable pace.

Occasionally, there are games that do not have explicit tutorials, and it is desirable to design a more formal lesson for learning the game. Ideally, this is done with an instructor demonstrating gameplay on a computer and projecting the display onto a screen. If there is sufficient time, beginning with only the instructor playing and students observing and taking notes makes for the gentlest learning curve. It is also effective to have students observe the instructor take a step in the game, then follow along on their own computers. If a projector is not available, an instructor can give step-by-step instructions that each computer user follows.

If the teacher is comfortable with the game, she can deliver this formal training. This is also an opportunity to call on student experts. With a bit of preliminary planning, a student or students can teach their classmates how to play the game quite well. Under these circumstances, the teacher should supervise carefully to ensure that the expert is presenting the information in a way that works for the class, and that the class is following along. In practice, it is a good idea to remind the class that you will be moving together for purposes of instruction. Time is precious, and the most effective way to make sure all students have at least a core set of skills with a game is to work in close step during initial sessions. To aid in this, those who are already familiar with the game or the genre should be charged with helping their peers acclimate. Box 4.7 gives a rough outline of the initial steps for game training.

Box 4.7 BASIC OUTLINE FOR INITIAL GAME TRAINING

I. Prepare Class

A   Model game ahead of time.
B   Instruct students to follow along with the teacher. The teacher will demonstrate on the instance of the game displayed on the projector, and then students follow on their own computers.
C   Before starting the game, introduce the game, provide students with the main goals of gameplay in print, and discuss the main goals.

II. Begin with Everyone on the Game's Starting Menu

A   Give explicit instruction on whether the default settings for the game are to be used or students need to adjust some of the settings. As a general rule, set the difficulty to easy the first time playing the game.

III. First Steps of the Game

A   Introduce students to the game interface.
B   Ask students to refer back to the stated goals for the game. Proved a basic strategy for gameplay and go through the steps.
C   Have students go through a set of defined steps then stop for questions and to check for comprehension.

Even when the game contains explicit tutorials, it may be advantageous for a teacher to train students herself. The advantage is that the teacher can focus the learning sessions on the key elements of gameplay that students should experience, which may not be the same thing as the key elements presented by in-game tutorials. To take one example: *Rome: Total War* has a tutorial campaign that begins by briefly introducing the player to the campaign map of Italy and the Mediterranean then quickly thrusting the player into a tactical battle tutorial. Players can spend considerable amounts of time trying to win the battle before they are returned to the campaign map to learn about managing cities, recruiting units, and other elements of imperial administration. If the goal is to have students learn both about Roman warfare and imperial administration in-depth, the tutorial is appropriate. If, on the other hand, a teacher opts to focus only on imperial administration, considerable classroom time can be saved by avoiding the tutorial and directly teaching students how to play the imperial campaign. Direct training can make a more complex game manageable. When learning to play *Civilization*, students can be taught to automate certain tasks, such as workers' efforts to improve terrain surrounding cities, and allow the computer advisors to handle others, like scientific research. When playing a city-builder, students can be taught to ignore the most advanced structures and focus on the core buildings needed for a functioning community. These sorts of tips and focused training sessions significantly reduce the initial challenge of playing, allowing students to devote themselves more easily to mastering basic gameplay. When in doubt, err on the side of explicitly teaching students to play.

Along with instruction in the basic mechanics of the game, students playing more complex games, particularly open-ended ones, will benefit greatly from receiving a set of initial steps to take to ensure at least limited initial success in-game. City-builders, for example, tend to disintegrate into unwinnable situations quickly if no balance is struck between the size of the population, the rate at which necessary resources are produced, and the availability of amenities. One can easily find oneself out of resources and unable to build further. If time is no object, learning to play through a series of errors, learning what not to do, can be very effective. Rarely are teachers so fortunate in terms of time, however. Students can be effectively brought up to speed and hours can be saved in the learning process if, during initial instruction, a set of concrete steps is provided that will lead to basic success in the early stages of the game, a sort of equilibrium from which they can venture forth and explore the game more fully. Using the city-builder as an example again, one could have students begin the game by constructing a specific set and number of buildings within specified areas. Once they have followed the directions and established a simple working city, they can branch off on their own and take more risks.

Closely related to providing students with a set of early gameplay strategies is the need to communicate clearly the winning conditions for the game. While it should usually be unimportant whether a student wins a game, understanding the winning conditions in a game makes decision-making in a game clearer for a student and, for the competitively attuned, more engaging. The converse is also true. Students playing large scale grand strategy games such as *Civilization* can be puzzled by the gameplay initially. They can be told how to settle, manage, and develop cities, and given a strategy for planting a string of cities early on in the game. Some players will find the exercise baffling, if not pointless, however, unless they are clear that victory in the game is predicated upon forming a large civilization consisting of many cities with large populations. When the game is more open ended, as, for example, many city-builders are, provide students with an in-game goal to help guide them—growing the city to a certain size, for example, or generating a certain amount of trade.

When students are comfortable with the basics of playing the game, the next step is to provide a learning environment where they can and do consider the historical models in the game. Students should explore and analyze the game in detail, try out different strategies, note and discuss their observations, and keep foremost in mind the ways the game does and does not represent reality. Often this is most efficiently achieved by selecting the scenario students will play and setting goals. While micro-managing students' play experience is not an optimal strategy, neither is creating a scenario so open ended that students flounder. Left to their own devices, children and young adults are not categorically more likely to explore thoroughly a game's inner workings through freeform play than anyone else, or at least, not when the game is assigned rather than one they have chosen to play for fun. Having clear goals for students will keep them focused and guide them to the sorts of gameplay that will help them analyze the game. So, for example, if a game is open ended, like city-builders, *Civilization*, or *Total War* games, set basic goals—support a population of 50 inhabitants, build five cities and reach the Middle Ages, conquer five provinces, and so on.

Forming Play and Observation Groups

While students are learning to play the game, particularly a game of any complexity, it is best to devote initial in-class play time to learning the game rather than analyzing it. Flooding students with questions about the models in a game when they are not even comfortable playing the game can create an emotionally overwhelming experience, and overwhelming experiences are rarely productive learning experiences. Once students are familiar with gameplay, however, it is time to move into analytical activities.

Though there will be exceptions, it is often most effective not to have students play individually when in class, at least once they have initially learned how to play and are at the stage of observing how the game works. Assigning students to play the game in groups creates a far more effective learning environment for several reasons. First and foremost, employing play teams emphasizes development of collaboration skills. In addition to being an important skill in its own right, collaboration allows students to help one another when playing, pooling their talents and insights. Furthermore, when teams, rather than individuals, play a game, the experience is more easily structured as a lab experience complete with observation and discussion; individuals run the risk of being too engrossed to make observations along the way. Finally, when students work in teams, strengths are maximized and weaknesses mitigated; in practice, this reduces the pressure on any one individual to master the game.

Teams of three students tend to be highly effective. In this configuration one person acts as the controller of the game while the others contribute to gameplay decisions and take steady observation notes. The observers keep the necessary notes that will serve for later reflection and analysis while the controller guides the game. Groups of more than three members can be used; the more members in a group, however, the more likely some will be more distracted and disengaged. This can be remedied somewhat by assigning explicit individualized tasks for each observer. For example, each student taking notes can focus on a specific aspect of game play, or develop some historical questions, while another manages the team of player and observers.

Logging Observations and Making Content Notes/Answering Content Questions

Once students have played the tutorial and are comfortable with basic gameplay, it is time to start recording observations, making content notes, and answering questions about content set by the teacher. If students do play the game on their own in class, remember to have them pause every so often and make observation notes—without a reminder it is too easy to get engrossed in a game and forget to make notes. Providing concrete goals for a session of gameplay and observation can facilitate the process. For example, students may be required to turn in a certain number of observations, historical questions, and criticisms in a game session. These observations will serve as important points of data for later reflection and analysis.

The basic purpose of the logs is to record observations that aid in comprehension and serve as evidence for the game's interpretation. Providing guidelines for notes, a set of topics and questions, can be helpful at this point (Box 4.8). No one instantly becomes an effective note-taker when a game is the subject matter, so clear expectations help facilitate the

Box 4.8 SOME STANDARD GAME OBSERVATION QUESTIONS

1   What are the stated or implied objectives for the game?
2   Who are the developers of the game?
3   What is the genre of the game?
4   What is the player's role and goal in the game? How does one succeed in the game? How can one fail?
5   What are the obstacles the player faces?
6   What tools/resources/decisions can the player use and make to overcome obstacles?
7   What is the scale of the game? Does the player represent one individual, a group, or a semi-omnipotent leader? How many real-world individuals do individual models in the game represent?
8   What are the main variables that determine success or failure in the game? How do these variables seem to be calculated?
9   What are the primary kinds of gameplay (input controls, etc.)?
10   How does a player know whether they are winning or losing? Does the game offer feedback in terms of a score, losses of territory, resources, or support from other characters?
11   How difficult is the game to play and what is the relationship between the difficulty of the game and the subject matter?
12   How accurate is the game? To what extent does accuracy seem to be an important goal of the developers?
13   What are the aesthetics of the game and how do they contribute to the game? Consider:
   a   artwork;
   b   music;
   c   any full motion video.
   Are the aesthetic elements integrated into the core gameplay or superficial?

process. Most points of interest are fair game for the observation log, but providing these general questions to students before their gameplay session serves to focus their efforts effectively. These are some of the standard questions to guide observation of any simulation game. Depending on the goals of the teachers, some can be emphasized and others omitted.

It can also be very effective for a teacher to develop worksheets with lists of specific terms and content questions to draw from the game. These aids can greatly help students narrow down the critical aspects of the game.

Serious/persuasive games call for a few additional questions. Since these games are intentionally designed to educate, inform, or persuade, they raise questions about the kinds of learning the games actually foster. Hence the following additional questions:

Box 4.9 SOME ADDITIONAL OBSERVATION QUESTIONS FOR SERIOUS GAMES

14 What kinds of learning did the designers want players to experience? (examples: knowledge, skills, problem-solving, empathy or understanding)
15 What kinds of learning do you think most players actually will experience?
16 To what extent are real-world kinds of skills, knowledge, and problem-solving required to succeed at core gameplay?

ANALYTICAL ACTIVITIES: FOSTERING LAB-STYLE INQUIRIES

Purposeful analysis, reflection, and debriefing are critical to learning with simulation games effectively. A simulation game by itself is only a tool, and playing one is not enough to make for a meaningfully serious learning experience in history. If students play a game without taking time to reflect on their experiences and analyze gameplay, most of the critical learning potential in the exercise is lost. It is the chief characteristic of analytical thinking to break down topics and objects into their constituent parts and relationships, topics and objects that are often left well enough alone by the uncritical. The trick is to get students into an analytical mode so that they deconstruct elements of the simulation, and, in doing so, engage in a meaningful inquiry about the past. Careful consideration and planning are required to encourage this kind of analysis; a game cannot achieve this kind of inquiry on its own.

Applying the principles of inquiry learning is an excellent means of getting students to analyze the models in a simulation. Essentially, students are presented with a series of problems that they must solve by turning to the simulation game. This way, students are encouraged to dig more deeply into the simulation's models, considering how the simulation works and exploring the ramifications of the models for understanding the world. These sorts of inquiry learning tasks can help students develop skills and strategies for solving problems. This is also an excellent opportunity to encourage students to engage in interdisciplinary work by using basic algebra and arithmetic to reconstruct game models, a task that can help develop procedural literacy. The following tasks offer some examples:

Box 4.10 SAMPLE INQUIRY QUESTIONS ABOUT GAMEPLAY

Pre-modern city-builders

Determine the relative size of agricultural fields to city buildings on the map and calculate the amount of land needed to support the city in the game.

How is the food supply calculated each month and how much food does each type of food source provide to the granary?

How is happiness calculated?

Modern city-builders

Determine the population of the city and

1   Calculate the amount of actual electricity the city would consume on a regular basis and the amount supplied by each power source.
2   Research: Is this an accurate representation of modern power plant capacities?

City-builders

Experiment with raising and lowering taxes. What are the results? Compare the results to the tax rates in comparable societies.

Nation-builders

Determine how long it takes a military or trade force to reach a given destination, and what the average speed of travel is. Does this fit within plausible parameters?

War

Determine the speed and distance which an army can travel by measuring movement allowances and comparing in-game maps to real-world maps.

Trade

Calculate the travel times of ship and land transportation in the game to various destinations. Construct average speeds. Compare to historical data.

Determine what the most and least valuable commodities are by weight and compare to historical data.

Determine the most profitable trade route in profit/mile or profit/time.

Political Tactics (*A Force More Powerful*)

How much would it cost in the real world to conduct the following tactics effectively in terms of money and personnel:

- publishing and distributing literature;
- creating and distributing T-shirts with slogans;
- holding a mass vigil or march.

Political Tactics (*Political Machine*)

What is the most efficient electoral strategy possible that requires traveling the smallest amount?

If one's opponent wins Texas and California, which three states does your candidate have to win in order to be elected?

Another good problem-solving exercise is to present students with the kinds of problems they could face in gameplay and ask them to craft strategies needed to solve the problem. See Box 4.11 for example.

A third type of analytical exercise is to apply historical knowledge to in-game situations and study how the game's models respond. The structure of such activities is reasonably straightforward. Students learn about historical strategies through classroom activities, independent research, or both. They then attempt to apply their strategic knowledge to the game. Finally, they observe how the strategies worked in the game and offer an analysis. Activities of this sort can range from reconstructing historical cities to following historical military, political, and even non-violent protest strategies. Any historical strategy or course of action that can be articulated and executed in-game provides a good opportunity for this type of activity. Exercises of this sort should be followed by an opportunity for reflection through discussion or writing.

BOX 4.11 GAME SCENARIO PROMPTS FOR FORMING STRATEGIES

City-builders

You are informed that your granary is empty or food stocks are low. What steps must you take to diagnose the problem? What are some possible solutions?

Your settlement has excellent supplies of (*name of resource*) but no access to (*name of resource*). How will that affect the structures in your settlement? Is it necessary to secure access to (*name of resource*)? If so, what might be done to secure access?

Civil unrest/rioting/fires are plaguing your city. What are some immediate, long term, and preventative measures that can be used to address the problems?

Nation-builders

You want to preserve your independence from a much more militarily powerful neighboring nation. What are your options?

Your nation's budget is unbalanced and you must reduce spending and/or increase revenue significantly. What are the factors that you must consider before deciding where and how to make up the shortfalls in the budget?

Trade Games

Develop a list of cargoes and ports for high risk/high profit trading and low risk/low profit trading. Under what circumstances would each be the sounder course of action?

War

What is the most efficient route to invade/attack (*name of territory*)?

Suppose you have to defend (*name of territory*). Where are the most effective defensive positions? Why?

Political Tactics (*Political Machine*)

Suppose your candidate's approval rating is down in the states of California, Ohio, and New Jersey. There is one week left to campaign; where should the candidate go, and what should they do?

Political Tactics (*A Force More Powerful*)

You have a highly enthusiastic and dedicated, but unskilled force of protesters for your movement. What are the best ways to take advantage of the assets of your group and offset the weaknesses?

PLANNING FOR REFLECTION AND DEBRIEFING

Just as students need to be encouraged to analyze simulations, they must also be given ample time and opportunity to reflect and debrief on their experiences. In practice this means that once students have learned to play the simulation game at a reasonable level, they must be required to take regular breaks for reflection and analysis. In addition, after every play session students need an opportunity to discuss, or at least write about, their observations and insights. When students are playing the game in teams, allocating a bit of time midway through a class period and at the end of class for them to stop playing and discuss what happened during the session is effective. When students are completely done playing the game, or at regular intervals for longer games, provide more formal opportunities for them to discuss and form conclusions on major issues in groups, with the teacher serving as a guide.

Too often, recitation, where the teachers asks questions and receives responses from individual students in a whole-class setting, is mistaken for discussion. Certainly there are times when it is appropriate for the teacher to moderate class discussion, particularly when it is necessary to ensure that certain topics are addressed and certain items of evidence are brought to light. When part of the goal is to foster the development of authentic discussion skills and provide opportunities for each student to have their own voice, however, students, ideally, should work together in small groups to discuss the questions and record their conclusions. Meanwhile, the teacher moves around the classroom, engaging groups when helpful or necessary. Otherwise the teacher simply monitors that productive conversations are taking place about the game. Recent research has suggested that students can also benefit from having online text-based discussions through forums (Guiller, Durndell, & Ross, 2008). When compared, both face-to-face and online discussions have somewhat different strengths. Face-to-face discussions tend to promote more clarification of issues and free exchange of ideas, but less focus on explicit reasoning and use of evidence. Online text-based discussion, on the other hand tends to produce increased evaluation of, and explicit reference to evidence in support of claims. This research suggests a powerful configuration for learning is for students to follow up a face-to-face discussion segment with an online discussion segment, the former to clarify ideas and brainstorm, the latter to focus more precisely on the evidence and reasoning.

Designing meaningful questions about a simulation and providing access to relevant evidence is central to fostering effective discussions. Most of the questions presented previously in the chapter will serve as excellent reflection questions. Generally an effective set of questions requires students to draw from specific details of the game in order to draw higher level conclusions about the game. Box 4.12 offers some more examples.

Box 4.12 SAMPLE GAME REFLECTION QUESTIONS

Life Management

What are the primary challenges that families in developing nations face today and what are the means for overcoming these challenges?

City-builders/Nation-building

There are many different positions on the role taxes should play in a society and whether taxes should be higher or lower in general. What is the game's position on the relationship between taxes, happiness, and productivity? How are taxes, happiness, and productivity measured in the game? What are the potential range of values for each and how do they change in relation to each other?

Nation-building

Does the game suggest that certain forms of government are more effective for meeting goals than others or, perhaps, that certain forms of government are categorically better than others? Consider the different types of governments available and their specific effect on aspects of gameplay.

Presidential Campaign Games

One common criticism of presidential candidates is that they are not completely truthful and completely consistent in the views they present on the campaign trail. Another related criticism is that they do not fulfill all the promises they made while campaigning (things they said they would do as president, they did not do).

According to the game, is it possible for a candidate to be elected who is:

- completely truthful?
- completely consistent in their stands on issues?
- largely unwilling to make promises?

Support your answer by referring to how a candidate actually determines voters' stances and gains support in each state in the game. If the answer is no, what does that suggest about the U.S. presidential election system? Does it force candidates, if they wish to succeed, to be less than completely forthright about their beliefs and plans? Does the system corrupt?

In general there are several kinds of questions one can ask about a simulation game. Questions about content concern the information the game presents about the past and how it operated. There are also questions of interpretation and accuracy. These ask whether the presentations of content are justifiable, supportable by valid evidence. Questions of extension and implication on the other hand, ask students to consider, if the simulation model is true, what can students expect or predict? Finally, there are questions about aesthetics and gameplay that include considerations of graphics, text, and music, what the player can do, and what feedback they receive from the game as a result. These questions focus primarily on analyzing the game as a form of media. The most effective debriefing questions will combine several of these categories, encouraging students to analyze and evaluate the simulation more thoroughly.

SELECTING AND STUDYING THE HISTORICAL EVIDENCE

In some cases the simulation unit may not incorporate an examination of independent historical evidence. There will be times when the teacher judges a simulation to give a reasonable presentation of an issue and, due to time or consideration of the learning objectives, wants students to spend most of their time learning from the portrayal of the past, and constructing an analysis of the game. Certainly, when time is tight, the teacher can run a critique of a simulation quickly and efficiently, pointing out in class discussion the more and less accurate elements of the simulation.

Granted it might be desirable, but it is not practical for students to dive deeply into the historical evidence for every topic and issue they study; this is as true when using simulation games as any other learning tool. When time permits and the goals of the unit allow, however, studying historical evidence on the topic simulated is part of a richer, more authentic historical study of a topic. Even if the goals prohibit spending too much time explicitly critiquing a game, it is a foundational part of historical understanding that accounts of the past should be corroborated through a multitude of sources.

If students are to read and analyze relevant historical evidence in conjunction with a simulation experience, there are equally valid reasons for scheduling this examination of evidence either before or after the gameplay. The advantage of waiting for the students to play the game before considering the evidence is that they will have experienced interacting with an engaging working model and both have a sense of context for the documents and be better able to raise research questions about the accuracy of the game. Playing the game first can also help uncover historical questions that will better focus research. On the other hand, researching before gameplay equips a student with, so long as the research has been conducted appropriately, valid historical evidence against which the game can be judged. If the primary goal is to reinforce familiarity with a specific set of evidence, however, researching before playing may be a more effective option. Either way, the criterion for useful evidence is straightforward: its ability to corroborate or challenge the game's interpretation.

Methods for introducing students to the available evidence can vary greatly from independent reading to direct instruction, depending on the type of evidence, age of students, and size of the class. One highly effective method for engaging and promoting critical discussion is to provide students with a set of readings from primary and secondary sources as homework for a day or two, then devote time in class to structured group discussions where students must complete an outline of what they can deduce from the evidence. Whenever possible students should access some primary sources, following the same hierarchy for evidence that historians use: though eyewitnesses must be interpreted with care, one cannot get closer to an event than to read, hear, or see the accounts of the eyewitnesses. Since many simulations incorporate large scale events and processes, how-ever, secondary sources will also need to be consulted to gain a broader understanding of the historical issues.

In addition to the resources provided by textbooks and print libraries, there are numerous excellent resources on the web for obtaining pertinent primary and secondary sources. A number of websites are dedicated to providing primary source materials for the study of the past. Google Books, and to a lesser extent Amazon.com, offer an extensive set of public domain and copyrighted, limited preview books that are searchable. Though the exact results will vary, searching here often yields a number of appropriate secondary source excerpts for researchers at a variety of age levels. One of the advantages of Google Books is that it can help reinforce core research skills. When a search term is entered, numerous instances of the term in various books are returned. In order to assess the usefulness of the excerpts, students will have to explore them and practice quickly skimming sections to see if there is relevant evidence within. This requires patience and an appreciation of the context of passages, excellent skills to instill in student researchers. Sometimes the research in Google Books will provide sufficient evidence; when more depth is needed the search tool can still help identify works to be obtained through a library or other means.

It is beyond the focus of this book to enter into a thorough exploration of history pedagogy as it concerns methods for developing defensible conclusions from valid evidence. Here, I would simply like to reiterate a main principle upon which this book is based. The job of a historian is to sift through evidence, engage in careful source criticism, corroborate and contextualize evidence, and provide an interpretation of the past that is meaningful. A classroom focusing on discipline-based learning will steer away from the concept of the "correct" interpretation and instead value defensible interpretations.

What does this mean in practice for students? First, that they be given ample opportunity to examine authentic documentary evidence and high quality secondary sources. Whenever possible they should discuss these sources with their peers. One of the major criticisms consistently levied at secondary school history is the overemphasis on textbook reading and the lack of sufficient opportunities to engage primary sources, the actual writings of the people of the past. By no means are all college level classes immune from this criticism. Students must be encouraged to critique the credibility of primary and secondary sources of evidence. Finally, students need to learn to corroborate the evidence in one source with that in others. Throughout these steps, the teacher needs to serve as a guide, a colleague historian offering hints, suggestions, opinions, and constructive criticisms that help students develop defensible interpretations of the past. Ideally, students will encounter a variety of sources of evidence and be required to think about the validity of each. It will be up to the teacher, ultimately, to determine the exact variety.

Debate and discussion are at the core of history. U.S. national curriculum standards recommend students frequently collaborate with their peers in small groups as they complete projects and engage in discussions. One way of accomplishing this is to place students in groups of four or so and assign members the following roles:

Manager   facilitates the smooth operation of the group as it completes its research tasks
Scribe   records the findings of the group
Presenter   delivers an oral presentation of the group's findings to the class
Lead historian   oversees that evidence is drawn from a variety of valid sources, and that the critical issues in the game are studied.

One or more class periods can be devoted to each group discussing the available evidence, forming conclusions, and presenting those conclusions to the rest of the class.

Box 4.13 shows a sample worksheet that guides students in analyzing evidence for *Rome: Total War*. With minor adjustments (changing the names and adding one or two more specific details) this worksheet serves equally well for any of more recent *Total War* games: *Medieval*, *Empire*, *Napoleon*, and *Shogun*.

Using this sheet, a session discussion, synthesizing, and drawing conclusions from historical evidence is followed by returning to the same questions during gameplay. Hence see Box 4.14 on the following page.

Sometimes the preliminary research questions need not be accompanied by a parallel observation sheet. This is the case in a simulation like *Energyville* where the preliminary research serves as a foundation for the great variety of power choices the player can make to power their future city (Box 4.15).

Box 4.13 PRELIMINARY RESEARCH QUESTIONS FOR *ROME: TOTAL WAR*

Total War: **Preliminary Historical Investigation**

Instructions: Before watching/playing the simulation, list what you would expect to find from an accurate simulation of Roman warfare. Use the evidence from the assigned sources or include valid sources from your own research. Cite your sources.

Weapons and Equipment

How were the Romans armed and armored?

Formations and Organization and Fighting Style

How were Roman infantry units organized? Were they in close order or open order (terms defined by the teacher)? Were they supposed to fight together as a team or more as individuals on the same side? To look at it another way, were individual Roman infantrymen supposed to stand out? How did Roman infantry fight? Did they fight as individuals or a team? How effective were the weapons and equipment?

Role of the General

What do you think the role of the general was in Roman battles? Would a general have had a great deal of control over his troops (remember, they could number in the 1,000s)?

Role of Casualties and Morale

What determined whether a unit could or could not fight any longer? Did units lose the ability to fight primarily through a loss of morale, a loss of soldiers, or a combination?

Box 4.14 *ROME: TOTAL WAR* **GAME OBSERVATION QUESTIONS TO FOLLOW RESEARCH**

Total War: **Playing, Observing, and Critiquing the Simulation**

Instructions: As you watch the simulation, take notes on the aspects that seem accurate or inaccurate based on what you have noted from the historical evidence. Use the following questions to guide your criticism.

Weapons and Equipment

Does the simulation accurately model the weapons and equipment of a Roman legion from the late third century BCE? List any accuracies or inaccuracies.

Formations and Organization and Fighting Style

- How are troops organized in the simulation?
- Are they in close order or open order?
- Do they fight together as a team or more as individuals on the same side?
- How effectively do they follow commands?
- How effectively do they move and change formation?
- Do you think the soldiers are realistic in the way they follow commands, move, and change formation? (*To judge this imagine how real human beings would fare in the same circumstances and remember—for real human beings this was not a game played in a relaxed setting.*)

Role of the General

How accurately does the game portray the role of a general in ancient Roman warfare? (*Remember that the player is in the role of the general. Does the player have information or control that a real general might not have had? Does the simulation place any limits on the control the general has that seem realistic?*)

Role of Casualties and Morale

What determines whether a unit can or cannot fight any longer in the simulation? How many casualties can a unit suffer in the simulation without fleeing? How often do units fight till they are completely destroyed?

Box 4.15 PRELIMINARY RESEARCH QUESTIONS FOR *ENERGYVILLE*

Chevron's Energyville: **Preliminary Investigation**

Instructions: Before watching/playing the simulation, list what you would expect to find from an accurate simulation of fueling a modern city. Use valid, clearly cited sources from your own research. Cite your sources.

Power Needs of a Modern American City

Select at least four different cities of different sizes. Indicate the population of each and the amount of energy consumed by the city.

What percentage of U.S. energy needs are currently met by each of the following sources of power? What are the benefits and costs and risks of each type of power both short term and long term?

- fossil fuels;
- hydropower;
- nuclear;
- natural gas;
- solar;
- wind;
- biomass;
- hydrogen.

To craft research questions like this, examine the core features of a game and pull out elements whose real-world counterparts can be researched.

★ ★ ★ ★ ★

Once students have learned to play a simulation and have had sufficient opportunity to observe and reflect upon it, teachers should move to more formal assessments, providing opportunities for students to engage in more elaborate description, analysis, evaluation, and creation. The following chapter surveys some of the many possible forms for more formal learning exercises and assessments.

CHAPTER 5

Putting It All Together

Learning Exercises, Assessments, and Sample Lesson Plans

The goal of simulation play in a history class is to enhance the ways that students study, analyze, and interpret human systems in the past (and present); assignments and assessments linked to simulation games should be designed accordingly. The exercises in this chapter provide examples of the many kinds of effective learning activities that can be designed. There is no one type of activity that is uniquely suited to promoting and assessing a student's learning in a lesson involving a simulation game. Analytical papers, reflective essays, formal and informal presentations, creative writing exercises, small group discussions, and many other types of learning activities all offer opportunities to critique the models found within a simulation, work with the historical content of a simulation, and form valid generalizations about the past. Some of these exercises are most suitable as homework exercises or as formative steps along the way to a larger summative assessment. Ultimately, each teacher must determine the combination of types, lengths, and weights of assessments that will meet the learning needs of their students.

Recent position statements by the National Council of Social Studies and National Council of Teachers of English have stressed the importance of training students to access, interpret, critique, and create new media. It may be helpful to consider what is meant, in this context, by new media. As opposed to what may be termed established media, much of which has been present for centuries, all of which was present for the majority of the twentieth century, new media forms—sometimes called twenty-first-century media—are those associated with digital communications, particularly those over the Internet. Table 5.1 provides some examples.

Table 5.1 Examples of established media and new media

Established media	New media
Printed texts and images	Digital text: blogs, wikis, forums, email, chat, texting, hypertext, webpages
Hard copies (on film or in print) of photographs	Digitally created, edited, altered, or enhanced images
Artworks or photographs of artworks	
Film	Digitally created, altered, or enhanced video and mash-ups
Taped audio recording	Podcasts and other digital audio recordings
	Interactive fiction
	Video games

Going further, the relationship between established and new media sources and publications in students' work can be broken down, for convenience's sake, into three broad categories:

- Using information and evidence from established forms of media (especially print) to create products of established media. For example, researching a topic using print resources in a library and writing a persuasive essay.
- Using information and evidence from new media (digital) to create new media products. For example, creating a website that provides an analysis and links to other websites, creating a digital video by editing and compiling a variety of online videos, or publishing a series of blogs that comment on the latest headlines from news webpages.
- Using a combination of established and new media to create a variety of established and new media products.

The exercises described in this chapter are intended to go beyond simply looking at simulation games as a form of new media to developing more savvy critics and creators of multimedia information. They offer a variety of established and new media products that can help students enhance their own media literacy as they work on developing their skills as historians, writers, and thinkers. Thus, these exercises are philosophically consistent with the educational imperative to help this and future generations of students learn to interpret and create a wide variety of established and new media effectively.

Before digging in, it is worth considering again the content basis of these exercises a bit more carefully, the problems posed by historical simulations. There are two main types of problems, in the sense of intellectual puzzles, that simulation games present to those studying them. The first type incorporates problems of content. These are the historical issues that a simulation raises and models, the questions of how and why people in the past acted in certain ways and not others. They are directly raised by gameplay; to put it another way, they are what the simulation is about. So, for example, life management games present problems involved with successfully using a family's resources; city-builders present problems of satisfying the needs of inhabitants given finite resources and limited space; trade games pose the problems of profiting in a supply-and-demand economy, and all games raise the issue of how to weigh alternatives in a world of scarcity and conflicting goals. Problems of interpretation compose the other type; they are considerations of how accurately the game represents the problems of content. The two are rarely wholly distinct. In the classroom, however, these types often get separated to simplify, and in doing so better facilitate, analysis and discussion.

To aid in planning, the exercises below employ the terms "content" and "interpretation/evaluation" to refer to the different types of problems. As noted above, however, the two are never completely divorced. When studying simulation games, students can beneficially consider both kinds of problems and engage in exercises that address each. Teachers should seize opportunities, either way, to remind them of the fundamental connection between epistemology and the content of history. To put it another way, teachers should ask their students regularly how they know what they claim to know, not only when it comes to simulation games, but all representations of the past.

A NOTE ON CREATING RUBRICS FOR ASSESSMENT

It is one thing to design a learning activity and another to assess it. When it comes to the more subjective work that is characteristic of high level history assessments, individual teachers can vary greatly in how they assess work. Still, one of the hallmarks of an effective assessment is clarity: as much as possible, students should know the categories and standards within each category that their teacher will use to assess their work. Crafting assessment rubrics that are precise, clear, and not cumbersome is something of an art itself, and teachers will vary in the ways that they phrase their standards for grading. Therefore, this chapter provides suggestions for rubric categories and standards rather than complete rubrics. This approach recognizes that teachers can benefit from seeing the important aspects of

Table 5.2 General format for suggested rubric categories and standards

Category	Standards
Name of a component of the overall grade (for example "Grammar and mechanics," "Design," "Argument," etc.	A description of the standards for excellent work in this category. (For example "Writing is grammatically and mechanically correct with the exception of a few or no typographical errors; Spell check has clearly been used carefully.")

assessing these works presented, but will ultimately end up designing rubrics that meet their own needs and are consistent with their own styles. When suggestions for rubric categories and standards are provided for assessments in this chapter, they follow the format indicated in Table 5.2.

Again, these are only guidelines to help teachers craft their own rubrics. Teachers who wish to develop rubrics based on the samples in this chapter will want to articulate standards for less-than-excellent work for each category and determine the weight of the various categories in determining the overall assignment grade.

CREATING VOCABULARY LISTS, CONTENT LISTS, AND WORKSHEETS

It is critical to take historical games fundamentally as interpretations that, like all interpretations, need corroboration from historical sources. Indeed, it is very difficult to justify the time and potential expense of a simulation as a learning tool when the goal is no more than to provide students with items of information rather than foils for analysis and debate: vocabulary, for example, the political geography of a country or the number of electoral votes Iowa has. It does not follow logically, however, that teachers and students should intentionally ignore core factual information that is part of a simulation game. Simulations are at their best illustrating systems and presenting interpretations, but both of these require the inclusion of specialized terminology and accurate historical content. Each simulation game will present terms and items of information that are critical to the topic of study. Identifying these terms ahead of time, providing them to students in list form, and assessing the extent to which students have learned to use these terms is an important part of teaching through simulation play. Care, of course, must be taken by the teacher to make sure that students are guided through the more and less accurate aspects of game content when they are treating the game more as a source of information about the past than as a text to be interpreted.

In addition to developing lists of content and vocabulary by playing the games directly, teachers can consult several other resources. Manuals for commercial strategy games often provide an excellent overview of content. Though physical manuals are becoming a rarity, most game disks contain a digital manual in PDF format. In addition, a number of strategy games contain in-game guides that contain a substantial amount of historical information. *Civilization*'s "civilopedia," for example, is an in-game encyclopedia that lists all units, inventions, wonders, scientific advances, and more in the game and includes succinct historical overviews for each entry. Each game in the *Total War* series also contains reference sections with detailed overviews for each building and unit. Many city-builders follow suit.

THE ESSENTIAL GAME BLOG/JOURNAL

The key to gaining familiarity with a game and its internal historical models is regular play and reflection. It is advantageous for students to keep a game journal with dated entries each time they play. Collecting reflections together into a journal—which need be no more elaborate than a composition book or a series of pages in a notebook—or its twenty-first-century analog, the blog, can add helpful formality to the reflective process, allows teachers to monitor and learn from students' ideas, and provides each student with a record of observations that can serve as data for more formal assignments. Blogging frequently helps keep students involved with game content and, equally as important, keeps them articulating their ideas in writing, an important practice for developing stronger writing skills.

If students have access to computers, styling the journal as a blog, regardless of whether the material is ever posted, provides an authentic model for writing about games. Taking this one step further, students can create actual online blogs so long as this is in accordance with the policies of the school, school board, state, etc. Be sure to get approval from school administrators before having students create blogs for a class, and be sure that student-created blogs do not violate school and local policies about student privacy. Currently, Wordpress (www.wordpress.com) and Blogger (www.blogger.com) are the leading providers of free space and software for blogging. Blogs such as Ian Bogost's *Joystick 101*, *2¢ Worth*, and *Wired Magazine's Game Blog* provide good examples of formal blogs focused on games and education. The basic standard for blog entries is that, while they may not be typographically perfect, they demonstrate the author has a command of written English. To put it another way, some formal blog authors may accept looking careless or rushed, but not fundamentally unskilled or unclear as writers. This practical standard works well for student journals.

Though a blog entry does not always need to be a response to a particular writing prompt, providing some guidelines for writing can help generate more productive entries. Take the following list:

1 What have been your experiences trying to play the game?
2 Describe your game session.
3 What was the role and goal of your assumed character in the game?
4 What challenges did your character face, and how successfully did your character overcome these challenges?
5 Describe one system the game employs.
6 Raise at least two questions about the past that your play-session inspired.
7 Does the game effectively demonstrate the key factors in the success or failure of the player?
8 Suppose you had to develop a plan of action in the real world based on the simulation's interpretation. What would your plan of action be and why?
9 Speculate: explain one aspect of the game that you think is historically accurate and offer reasons in support.
10 Speculate: suggest one aspect of the game that you suspect is historically inaccurate and offer reasons in support.

These prompts are arranged in a rough progression of complexity and include issues of content and evaluation. The first six prompts are particularly appropriate for one still learning to play the game. They allow the student to respond emotionally, descriptively, and analytically, acclimating to the game as they do so. This gradual approach can help students gain comfort with the game; the entries can also suggest to the teacher ways to make the students' experiences more productive by adapting future lessons and addressing stumbling points. At the other end of the list are questions that require more focused thought about the game as a historical model, questions that cannot be answered effectively without familiarity with the game.

Effective prompts to encourage students to consider the implications a particular game's model has on the real world can be crafted using formulas like "What does (*name of game*) suggest about (*topic*)?" Another useful phrasing is "If the way (*name of game*) portrays (*issue/topic*) is essentially accurate, what does this suggest about (*a related issue/topic*)?" Other variants follow the same pattern: they ask the student to assume something in the game, for sake of argument, is accurate and then extrapolate from that system to consider real-world past and present problems. Here are some examples designed to be open ended, and sometimes even provocative:

- What does *Rome: Total War* suggest were the causes of Roman imperialism in the Republic?
- What does *A Force More Powerful* suggest are the strengths and limitations of non-violent protests as a means of countering injustice and oppression?
- If *Third World Farmer* portrays the general problems people face in developing nations, how might foreign aid money best be spent to improve the condition of farmers in developing nations?
- How independent could a medieval lord be with a manor of the type that can be created in *Stronghold 2*? What insight does the manor system in *Stronghold 2* offer for why medieval Europe was politically, legally, and economically decentralized?
- Which form of government does *Civilization* suggest is most effective for managing a people?
- According to the *Political Machine*, what is the role of money in presidential campaigns? Is it likely for a person of modest means to win election to the presidency?

Again, the point here is to encourage students to think about the extent to which a simulation's models can address the legitimate problems posed in history classes. Remember, too, that all of these journal prompts can form the basis for formal and informal class discussions.

GAME DESCRIPTION, REFLECTION, AND ANALYSIS EXERCISES

These exercises encourage students to study the game in greater depth. They are designed to encourage analysis of how the game world works, serve to connect elements of content, and lay the foundation to consider a game's problems of interpretation. Beyond preparing for the high level critique of a simulation's interpretations, analysis exercises are valuable in their own right because they require students to think about content. They encourage thinking about the opportunities and limits that existed for humans in past situations. Just as it is somewhat artificial to separate content from questions of interpretation, it is also artificial to separate analysis exercises from critique exercises. Certainly, most of these game analysis exercises can be easily adapted into criticism exercises. The separation here is simply intended to reinforce an important point: formal scholarly critique requires a solid understanding of the available evidence, a foundation from which one can base one's criticisms. When training students to appreciate the difference between everyday emotional or aesthetic criticism and formal criticism, a primary rule is: Do not offer formal criticism without having referred to valid evidence. Following this rule, though a critical thinker will certainly form opinions about the realism of a game as they analyze it, they cannot offer a truly valid critique without reference to valid evidence; in practice this means research is needed.

Diagramming Game Systems

Since facilitating the understanding of dynamic systems is one of the strengths of simulation games, diagramming one or more systems in a game is a natural analytical exercise. Any number of diagram styles could be employed. For example, the following diagram template can be used for indicating the factors or processes that contribute to, or cause, a phenomenon in the game.

Figure 5.1 Simple causal diagram

In general, a process can be diagrammed as steps represented by shapes, with arrows indicating representing the direction of the process:

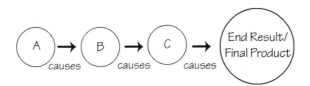

Figure 5.2 Another simple causal diagram

A supply chain can be represented in the same way. So, for example, given the prompt, "create a diagram of the food system in *CivCity: Rome* from the initial production of raw food resources to the consumption of food by city inhabitants," a chart like the following might be generated:

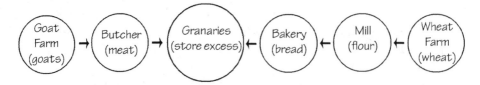

Figure 5.3 A simple causal diagram for food production in *CivCity: Rome*

Really, any game mechanic that can be broken into several components, whether steps in a process, related elements in a system, or components in a product, or factors in a major decision, can effectively be diagrammed.

There are myriad possible prompts for diagramming game systems. The following are just a few examples useful for current games, with minor modifications, to future games:

- Diagram three supply systems. Include each step in the chain and the process carried out at that step. (city-builders)
- What are the main factors that determine the size of a city/settlement? (*Civilization*; city-builders)
- What are the factors that influence whether a unit continues to fight in battle? (war)
- Diagram a system of ports and trade routes needed to supply a city with the following commodities: (*insert list*). (trade)
- What are the primary sources of income and expenditure for the nation and what are the benefits each expense provides? (nation-building)
- What are the main sources of income and expenditure for your family? (life management)

Diagrams of systems and processes like these help students reinforce that games are in fact systems, and analyze them accordingly. Cause-and-effect relationships are hypothesized in the process and the groundwork is laid to apply a game's historical models to problem solving and evaluate the game's models.

Annotating Screenshots for Description and Analysis

Screenshots, digital copies of game screens, provide a visually rich subject to analyze, and annotating them provides a way for students to demonstrate analytical skills independent of their formal writing skills. They also give students an opportunity to organize and articulate their thoughts about a game informally. As with other in-game analyses, these kinds of annotations help the student focus on problems of content. Annotated screenshots are effective as homework assignment prior to a larger more formal analysis or as the core of a formal analysis of content.

There are two basic types of annotation for a game screenshot that can be combined as desired. The first, considered here, describes the game's models, how it presents historical systems and content. It is a useful exercise for students to describe some of the models in a game early in their play time as a preliminary to critiquing the models. Given the prompt, "outline key components of a Democratic presidential candidate strategy using the electoral map in *Political Machine*," something like the following annotated screenshot might be created (see Figure 5.4).

The basic prompt for this type of exercise is something like this: "Annotate a screenshot of (*name of game*) so that the key elements of the simulation are presented." Any number of more specific prompts for screenshot annotations could be assigned; here are just a few examples:

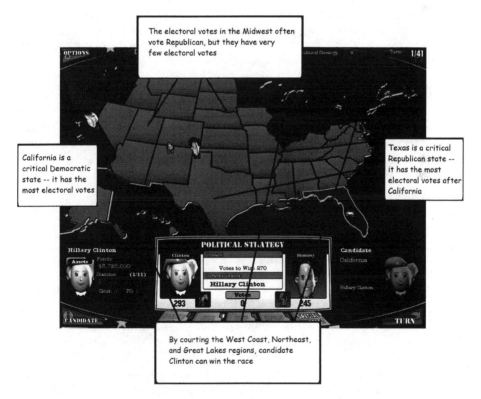

Figure 5.4 Sample of a hypothetical screenshot annotation of *Political Machine*
Credit: © Stardock Systems Inc.

- Annotate the main components of one or more supply systems. Note what each does and the order in which goods/service travel through each component. (city-builders)
- Annotate the city screen of your least productive city in *Civilization*. Note the key geographical features and resources surrounding the city and how they affect the productivity and growth of the city.
- Annotate a screenshot of the list of goods to be found in (*name of port city*). Explain why certain goods are more expensive than others and note the uses of these goods in the game. (trade)
- Annotate a screenshot that illustrates the geopolitical, diplomatic and military position of your nation/civilization in relation to others nearby. What advantages and disadvantages does your state have in relation to others? (nation-building)

These prompts should be accompanied by clear guidelines of how many annotations to include and the amount of detail expected (expressed in number of words/sentences, etc.).

Obtaining screenshots can be a simple or more involved process, depending on the game. Ideally on Windows PCs and Macs one can take a screenshot of a game simply by using the print screen function while playing the game—this involves pressing the Print Screen key in Windows or pressing Command-Shift-3 in Mac OS X. If the print screen function is disabled by the game, there are freely available programs for Windows and Mac OS X that allow the user to take screenshots of video games. An easier solution is to use one of the myriad screenshots posted online for most video games at review sites, fan sites, and the official game sites. While the exact screen the player wants to annotate may be unavailable this way, it is quick and easy for students to search the web for a screenshot of their game that best represents the areas they need to annotate. This method is a good compromise if making a custom screenshot is too difficult.

Analytical Essays on Core Game Models

Under the discussion of game journals/blogs it was noted that teachers can encourage students to consider the implications a particular game's model has on the real world by crafting appropriate blog prompts. Writing a formal essay analyzing how a simulation game functions is the next level on this path. Such essays can be valuable as a step toward critiquing a game, or in their own right as exercises of interpretation and analysis. Questions for these essays can be formed using the guidelines under blogging. Box 5.1 offers some examples of essay prompts for the *Civilization* series:

Box 5.1 ESSAY PROMPTS FOR ANALYZING *CIVILIZATION* GAME MODELS

Introduction

Civilization as a simulation game provides an interpretation of the creation and development of world civilizations. Pick one of the following areas of the simulation and write an essay on what the simulation suggests about this feature in the development of civilizations. This is not a critique of the accuracy of the simulation, but an analysis of what the simulation suggests about the past.

Geography and Resources

How does *Civilization* model the effects of terrain and natural resources on the growth of a civilization? What role does *Civilization* suggest geography plays in developing a strong prosperous civilization?

Governments (note you must examine the following types of government: despotism, monarchy, republic, democracy)

How does *Civilization* model the effects of different kinds of government on the growth and functioning of a civilization? What are the trade-offs involved in choosing different kinds of government? Does the simulation suggest some forms of government are better than others?

International Relations

How does *Civilization* model the relationships between different peoples/nations/governments? What kinds of diplomacy are available and what are the potential effects of these kinds of diplomacy? What are the trade-offs involved in diplomatic negotiations? Does *Civilization* offer a primary lesson about international relations?

Finances

How does *Civilization* model the financial resources of a civilization? What are the major sources of expense and income for a civilization in the game? What are the kinds of considerations and trade-offs a player must consider when making an effective financial policy/budget?

With a little practice, questions like those in Box 5.1 can readily be developed for any simulation following a format like "What does (*name of simulation*) suggest about (*name of real-world event/system/process*)?" or "How does (*name of simulation*) characterize (*name of real-world event/system/process*)?" Since these prompts task students to interpret a simulation game, the evidence supporting their conclusions should be drawn explicitly from elements of gameplay. Accordingly, key categories for a rubric are suggested in Table 5.3.

Table 5.3 **Some suggested rubric categories for a brief analytical essay**

Category	Standards
Grammar and mechanics	Writing is grammatically and mechanically correct with the exception of a few (or no) typographical errors; Spell check has clearly been used carefully.
Argument	Ideas are clearly connected using effective transitions and chronological markers. Causal connections between ideas are made clear.
Use of supporting detail from game	Abundant explicit, rich details (details that are specific enough to have clearly come from gameplay, not vague assertions) are used to illustrate the events in the narrative. (*Specifying a certain number of details can be very helpful.*)

Writing Narratives of Simulation Play Sessions— Constructing Hypothetical Chronicles of Game Events

An excellent creative writing exercise that allows students to focus on the content of a simulation game, practice developing a sequential narrative, and speculate about the thoughts of past peoples is the construction of a hypothetical chronicle. A hypothetical chronicle is a narrative of a gameplay session told from the perspective of a member of the culture simulated in the game looking back on the events that occurred during play. The heart of these narratives should be the core challenges students' assumed characters faced during the session: the achievements and setbacks they had, the goals they pursued, their motives, and their internal responses to events. Taking these elements from the game session, the student crafts a third-person narrative about the session. So for example, a narrative about the medieval manor-builder *Stronghold 2* might tell of the efforts of the lord to construct a castle able to withstand the assaults of nearby foes. A narrative about a railroad building game might recount the work and decisions involved in constructing the first rail line between Pittsburgh and Philadelphia.

A chronicling exercise helps students collect their thoughts about the game in a creative format. Writing a chronicle can help promote empathy for people in the situation studied, since the voice adopted is of a member of the culture. With a bit more planning, such an exercise can also help develop an appreciation for the ways authors from different cultures in the past—and even within the same culture—treated the telling of their people's stories. For example one could have a student chronicle a session of Roman history-themed game in the style of Livy, a Roman historian, emphasizing Roman virtue as a primary cause of Roman success. As a literary connection, a student could also be asked to write in the style of the Roman epic poet Virgil, emphasizing the role of the gods and human piety in Roman success. To give two more examples, one could narrate a political campaign in the style of a more conservative or liberal news organization, or write a mayoral speech for the anniversary of the founding of a city constructed in a city-builder. One could also turn to different perspectives writing a chronicle from the perspective of the defeated, those digital peoples the player's character has overcome. Table 5.4 provides suggestions for a rubric to assess these writings.

Table 5.4 **Some suggested rubric categories for a hypothetical narrative**

Category	Standards
Grammar and mechanics	Writing is grammatically and mechanically correct with the exception of a few (or no) typographical errors; Spell check has clearly been run carefully.
Style	Style approximates engaging scholarly writing by: • including varied, interesting, and appropriate word choices • avoiding repetitive phrasing and varying sophisticated phrasing • being precise and clear • using transitional words and phrases effectively as needed so that each sentence is connected to the next in an elegant fashion.
Narrative	Ideas are clearly connected using effective transitions and chronological markers. Causal connections between ideas are made clear.
Use of supporting detail from game	Abundant explicit, rich details (details that are specific enough to have clearly come from gameplay, not vague assertions) are used to illustrate the events in the narrative. (*Specifying a certain number of details can be very helpful.*)
Demonstration of character motivation	When the narrative indicates courses of actions taken, the game character(s)' motivation(s) and reasoning for those courses of action are provided in specific detail.

Creating Written Artifacts from Simulation Characters

Creating character writings is an exercise of historical imagination that encourages students to go deeper into the thoughts and ideas of a person in the game world. These are valuable exercises in historical thinking but also clearly tie in to some of the writing objectives in literature and writing courses, insofar as these activities require the exercise of empathy and imagination and a focus on characterization. Most historical strategy games assign a specific persona to the player, but often this character is defined in the barest of sketches in the game manual, the startup screens, or the initial cinematic sequence. For example:

- In the *Civilization* series the player is a specific historical leader from the civilization they choose (though with a millennia-long lifespan).
- In nation-building games the player is one ruler or a series of rulers.
- In city-builders the player is a generic mayor in modern versions, or a governor/lord in pre-modern scenarios.
- In *Total War* games the player is the head of a family or dynastic faction.
- In trade games the player is often an individual trader or head of a trading corporation.
- In life management games the player is either an individual or the guide for a family.

The player's character in these games is often a cipher simply justifying the player's role as decision-maker.

Character writing exercises invite the student to expand on the limited information about the character. Students use their experiences of playing the game to construct contextually appropriate written artifacts that illustrate the thoughts of the character. Letters, speeches, diary entries, treaties, virtually any type of written artifact that is relevant to the in-game content can be generated. The core criteria are (a) that the writing is based on a good understanding of the game and refers to explicit occurrences in the game world from play sessions; (b) the writing provides plausible details about the character's thoughts and feelings about the game-world occurrences; and (c) the style of written artifact and the way it references material from the simulation are appropriate to the character who created the artifact. A few possibilities for character writings include:

- personal letters from the player's character to a another in-game character;
- official records of supplies, manifests, etc.;
- a speech justifying a course of action;

Table 5.5 **Some suggested rubric categories for character writing**

Category	Standards
Grammar and mechanics	Writing is grammatically and mechanically correct with the exception of a few (or no) typographical errors; Spell check has clearly been run carefully.
Style	Author has convincingly and successfully adopted an assumed style appropriate for the character through word choice, sentence structure, and phrasing.
Use of supporting detail from game	Abundant explicit, rich details (details that are specific enough to have clearly come from gameplay, not vague assertions) are used to illustrate the events in the narrative (*specifying a certain number of details can be very helpful*).
Demonstration of character	The game character(s)' motivations, reasoning, and feelings are provided in specific detail in a manner appropriate for one from the time, place, and culture portrayed in the game

- a diary entry—a merchant sailing to a new land, perhaps, or politician sharing their ambivalence about a public course of action;
- a recorded oral interview (for games set in appropriate time periods);
- a sketch of an event, operation, or interesting sight;
- a cartoon parodying a historical aspect of the game.

A slightly modified form of this type of exercise can also turn the assumptions of the game on their head a bit by challenging students to write about the under-represented groups in the game rather than the main character. Games that involve conquest, for example, generally focus on the point of view of the player's polity. An artifact-creating exercise could involve writing a letter of protest from a city that had been conquered and enslaved by the player. A city-builder exercise could focus on a member of the city's less enfranchised rather than the leader. Players of *Medieval: Total War 2* could develop a personal diary for a princess required to undertake a political marriage.

GAME CRITICISM AND EVALUATION EXERCISES

One point worth repeating frequently is that, philosophically, it is inconsistent with the practices of expert historians to accept any source of information uncritically. So too, students should not be trained to accept the models in games uncritically. While there can be many plausible parts to a given simulation game, it is still critical that students learn early and often how to research and critique a game's models. The exercises that follow shift some of their focus off the content of the game and onto evaluating the defensibility of the content.

Brief Research and Analysis Assignments

For a quick exercise, students can find a valid article, webpage, or book segment that provides information on some aspect of the game. They read the source and provide a brief explanation (in writing or orally) on the contents and how it reflects upon the accuracy of that aspect of the game. For example, one could briefly research whether small farmers in developing nations are targeted to produce opium poppies as the game *Third World Farmer* suggests. As another example, one could examine the role of aqueducts in Roman cities and determine whether they were considered a standard element in Roman cities as *CivCity: Rome* suggests.

Giving students leeway to research an aspect of the game they choose lays the groundwork for an excellent class session analyzing a game. Each student will have a slightly different perspective on a feature of the game as determined by their choice of topic and research. Working together in class to combine these elements into a coherent critique of a game will help develop collaborative skills of discussion.

There are many online research tools available—see the appendices for some suggestions. It is particularly worth considering the use of Google Books and, in the future, other online resources that allow users to search books and obtain limited preview excerpts. Using a tool like this can be exceptionally helpful, for less advanced students learning the core of research, or any student tasked with a limited research assignment. Certainly, Google Books eliminates the need to pore through the books in a library, but that has never really been the core cognitive task in research anyway, regardless of the pride many of us feel for having made successful journeys through the stacks. The advantage of a tool like Google Books is that its millions of searchable excerpts enable students to pursue aspects of almost any topic that could possibly be raised by the simulation. Nor is it the case that the information is presented in a neat, digested package. Beyond the need to effectively identify and employ the most effective search terms, researchers could have tens or hundreds of book entries that match their searches. To find references to evidence that suitably supports their arguments requires scanning the works to find whether the information is relevant. This is a core research skill that requires awareness of the context of terms in a text and a clear understanding of the parameters of a research question. Table 5.6 shows some suggested rubric categories for a researched essay.

Table 5.6 **Some suggested rubric categories for a researched essay**

Category	Standards
Grammar and mechanics	Writing is grammatically and mechanically correct with the exception of a few (or no) typographical errors; Spell check has clearly been run carefully.
Style	Author has successfully employed the hallmarks of an engaging writing style by: • including varied, interesting, and appropriate word choices • avoiding repetitive phrasing and varying sophisticated phrasing • being precise and clear • using transitional words and phrases effectively as needed so that each sentence is connected to the next in an elegant fashion.
Argument	Author has written an effectively organized, clear, and compelling argument through the use of the following elements: • Thesis is clearly stated, precise, and dictates the contents of the essay. • Topic sentences are clear, precise, relevant to the main point, and dictate the contents of the paragraph. • Supporting evidence is clearly paraphrased or quoted from clearly identified, valid sources. Sources are properly cited. • Inferences move beyond restating evidence to explaining how the evidence supports the main point of the author. • Connection between ideas is clear due to effective and appropriate use of transitional words and phrases.
Research	Specify the source requirements in terms of • number • variety • type • need for corroboration.

Annotated Screenshots for Criticism and Evaluation

The primary distinction between annotating a screenshot for in-game analysis or evaluation is the types of notes made. The examples in Figure 5.5 illustrate some evaluative statements that could be made of games.

Depending on the needs for this exercise, the level of rigor can always be increased by requiring each annotation to cite specific sources of evidence.

Researching and Writing a Thesis Driven Essay Evaluating a Simulation

The length and format of an evaluation paper can range greatly depending on the student abilities and the desired learning goals. It is beyond the

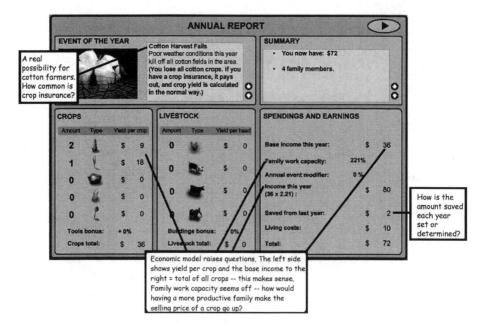

Figure 5.5 Sample of a hypothetical screenshot annotation of *Third World Farmer*
Credit: © Third World Farmer Team

scope of this book to delve deeply into the mechanics of assigning and evaluating historical writing. Here, let us consider the underlying principles that should be applied in a researched paper evaluating game models. Those interested in reading more about writing in the context of history education can consider the following works:

- *A Pocket Guide to Writing in History* by Mary Lynn Rampolla (Bedford/St. Martin's).
- *A Short Guide to Writing about History* by Richard A. Marius and Mel Page (Longman).
- *Writing History: A Guide for Students* by William Kelleher Storey (Oxford University Press).

1. Students Should, When Feasible, Craft Their Own Research Questions

It was noted early on that the ability to pose deep and meaningful questions within a discipline is an important component of thinking creatively, flexibly, and critically, and that simulation games can do an excellent job inspiring these kinds of questions. Unless there are compelling reasons not to do so, require students to develop their own research question in response to the simulation game. A general guide for forming such questions is: raise a question about the realism of some element of the simulation game, research the element, and argue whether the game is historically accurate in this respect. The advantage of forming and pursuing these questions, beyond the intrinsic cognitive value of the exercise itself, is that a student has a greater stake in investigating a question they have posed rather than one imposed upon them.

2. Students Should Consult Multiple Valid Sources of Evidence in Their Research and, When Possible, Balance Primary and Secondary Sources

Whenever possible, students should be encouraged to study the past through multiple sources of evidence and taught to corroborate the information in one source with that in others. Building expertise as a historian requires learning to hold evidence at arm's length, to take no printed word—or spoken word or image for that matter—at face value without considering the source of the evidence and without corroborating the evidence with that from other sources. No matter how skilled the historian, how gifted the stylist, how authoritative an account, effective historians are not in the practice of accepting one version of the past without checking it against other sources.

When it comes to the types of sources used, there is no avoiding the fundamental evidential basis of history. Historians cannot get any closer to a past event than to examine the testimony of eyewitnesses. This is not because eyewitnesses are always knowledgeable, unbiased, or even honest—no human is. Rather, one cannot get closer to an event than to look at the accounts of those who were there. Authentic historical analysis requires some consideration of primary sources, when those sources are extant. At the same time, valid secondary sources will prove critical to any large scale analysis of trends—the types of trends inherently modeled in many simulation games. For these aspects, valid secondary sources should be used.

3. Research and Written Criticism Should Focus on Major Aspects of the Game World, Not Minor Details

One of the history teacher's tasks is to help students learn to distinguish between the essential and trivial aspects of a representation of the past. Accordingly, the most meaningful analyses should focus on the major systems of a game, not the cosmetics. For example, spending all one's research time and writing simply to demonstrate the names of infantry types in *Rome: Total War* match the historical evidence will do very little to deepen a student's understanding of how the Romans lived and fought. Spending all one's efforts researching trade in the Caribbean only to note that a game did not include a certain handful of historical port cities similarly misses the point. Far better questions are how different units functioned together in battle, how geography influenced the specific development of civilizations, or how trade functioned in a given time and place. That said, teachers have an excellent opportunity with these kinds of assignments to differentiate assessments as needed by allowing some students to focus on concrete factual details and others to focus on larger scale processes. Boxes 5.2, 5.3 and 5.4, and Table 5.7 give some examples of research essay prompts that can be readily adapted to other simulation games.

Box 5.2 TEMPLATE FOR AN ESSAY ASSIGNMENT ON A SIMULATION GAME

Evaluating the Accuracy of *(name of simulation game)*

Introduction

The video game, *(name of simulation game)* offers an opportunity to view *(historical event/process/system)* as working systems. This raises the question, however, of how accurate a simulation of *(historical event/process/system)* the game actually is.

Your Task

Pick an aspect of the past that is represented in the game for which you have or can find valid historical evidence (you may use class materials). Identify the strengths and weaknesses of the simulation game's version of this aspect of the past and write a paper arguing how accurate the game is in portraying this aspect.

Some Possible Aspects to Critique

(some of these are broad and will need to be narrowed):

• List of topics with explanations

Requirements

- You will tackle this issue in a thesis-driven essay with a formal introductory paragraph and concluding paragraph.
- Minimum word count:
- Evidence must be properly cited and listed in a bibliography.

Note on Sources of Evidence

You will need to draw deeply from historical evidence and reasoning in order to evaluate the game. Your source materials must include:

- Readings from _____.
- Assigned primary source documents.
- Class notes.

Box 5.3 SAMPLE ASSIGNMENT FOR AN ESSAY ON *STRONGHOLD 2*

Medieval Manors and Castles: Evaluating the Accuracy of *Stronghold 2*

Introduction

The video game *Stronghold 2* offers an opportunity to view manor and castle life as a working system. Indeed, the game bills itself as "The Ultimate Castle Sim." This raises the question, however, of how accurate a simulation of medieval manor and castle life *Stronghold* actually is. *Your task*: Pick an aspect of medieval society that is represented in the game for which you have or can find valid historical evidence (you may use class materials). Identify the strengths and weaknesses of *Stronghold 2*'s version of this aspect of medieval society and write a paper arguing how accurate the game is in portraying this aspect.

Some Possible Aspects to Critique

(some of these are broad and will need to be narrowed):

The Relationship Between Lords And Peasants

- Is the reciprocal nature of the lord-peasant relationship represented well in the simulation?

- Are there limits in what a lord can do to peasants?
- How is the manor organized and kept orderly?

Medieval Agriculture

- How accurately does the agricultural system of *Stronghold 2* represent the medieval agricultural system?

Medieval Technology

- How accurately do the technologies of the simulation (ranging from raw material gathering and production to transport and communication) represent the technological abilities of medieval Europe?

Siege Warfare

- How accurately does the simulation represent the military features of castles and the nature of castle warfare?

Requirements

- You will tackle this issue in a thesis-driven essay with a formal introductory paragraph and concluding paragraph.
- Minimum word count: 600.
- Evidence must be properly cited and listed in a bibliography.

Note on Sources of Evidence

You will need to draw deeply from historical evidence and reasoning in order to evaluate the game. Your source materials must include:

- Assigned readings from J. Gies and F. Gies, *Life in a Medieval Castle*.
- Assigned primary source documents.
- Class notes.

Box 5.4 SAMPLE ASSIGNMENT FOR AN ESSAY ON *CIVILIZATION*

Civilization **as a Historical Interpretation**

Purpose

One of the most important skills of a historian is the ability to critique interpretations of the past. This involves:

- Identifying the key features of the interpretation.
- Considering how completely and well the interpretation explains why things happened in the past.
- Considering how well the interpretation fits the available evidence.

Analyze and evaluate the validity of one of the historical interpretations found in *Civilization*. First, select one of the topics from the list below or form your own (subject to approval). Then argue how historically accurate or inaccurate *Civilization*'s presentation of your topic is based on valid evidence.

To do this, you will need to have generated a great number of observations relevant to this topic during your playing sessions. You will also need to research this topic considerably.

Some Possible Aspects to Critique (you may pick your own)

1   The explanation of some civilizations' abilities to dominate and conquer others. What are the critical factors that enable some civilizations/nations to dominate others?
2   The technological development of civilizations. What is the relationship between culture and technology? Can the Iroquois, for example, develop fighter planes; is this historically accurate; what does this say about the game's interpretation of science/technology and culture?
3   The role of government in civilizations. Did the creators of *Civilization* have a bias toward certain types of governments? Are there factors in the game that make some governments more effective than others? Do these factors have real-world parallels?

Requirements

- You will tackle this issue in a thesis-driven essay with a formal introductory paragraph and concluding paragraph.
- Minimum word count: 800.
- Evidence must be properly cited and listed in a bibliography.

Note on Sources of Evidence

You will need to draw deeply from historical evidence as well as reasoning in order to evaluate the game. Your source materials must include:

- Class notes.
- Valid texts from Google Books.

Table 5.7 **Some suggested rubric categories for a formal researched essay**

Category	Standards
Argument, organization, and focus	• Thesis is clear, sophisticated, based on a thorough survey of evidence, and answers the question. • Thesis indicates the organization/contents of the paper. • Thesis is kept in focus throughout. • Strong topic sentences are related to the main argument and indicate the organization/contents of the paragraph. • The logical connections between paragraphs (and between sentences within a paragraph) are clear and relevant.
Support and reasoning	• Numerous examples (more than three per paragraph) of the strongest possible evidence are paraphrased or, when appropriate, quoted. • The source and context of the evidence is clear. • A legitimate citation for the evidence is given in parentheses after the evidence. • Evidence is drawn from a wide variety of sources. When the sources provided are limited, evidence is drawn from a wide sampling of the sources (e.g. not just one paragraph of a multi-page document). • Evidence chosen is among the best available and represents the whole. • Inferences move beyond restating the evidence to explaining how the evidence supports the main point. • Inferences and evidence answer the main question well.

Language, grammar and style	• Writing is grammatically and mechanically correct with the exception of a few (or no) typographical errors; Spell check has clearly been run carefully.
	• Style approximates engaging scholarly writing by:
	  – including varied, interesting, and appropriate word choices
	  – avoiding repetitive phrasing and varying sophisticated phrasing
	  – being precise and clear
	  – using transitional words and phrases effectively so that each sentence is connected to the next in an elegant fashion.

Formally Assessed Discussions

The task of formal analysis and evaluation can be achieved through formal discussions—discussions held according to certain criteria and used as a form of summative or formative assessment. Discussions are valuable both as exercises in productive collaboration between peers and as authentic examples of informed discussions experts in history hold. Though formal discussions can be conducted with the teacher in the room, these are often not truly free-flowing discussions between group members but greater or lesser forms of recitation. Most students are largely socialized to accept the teacher as authority figure in a discussion of academic content and, accordingly, tend to direct their comments to the teacher rather than truly discussing with peers. The goal for a formal discussion, however, should be for students to engage in open, unstilted exchanges of ideas, evidence, and reasoning with their peers. This can best take place when the teacher's presence in the class is minimized, if not removed altogether.

How then, is the teacher to observe and assess these discussions? There are two effective modes of structuring and assessing discussions without the teacher present. Both serve different purposes and can effectively be used separately and in combinations. The first is the recorded face-to-face discussion. In this form of exercise, a group of three to six students are provided a quiet place and a video camera or voice recorder. They spend anywhere from 20 to 50 minutes discussing a set of questions. Ideally, students will have had some time to prepare for the questions and bring their resources and notes; this way they will be equipped to have a more substantial conversation. The advantage of discussions of this sort is that they remove the teacher from the dynamic of the conversation. Students, consequently, are required to engage one another and not focus upon saying what they think the teacher wants to hear. This can result in some truly impressive examples of student engagement and intellectual responsibility. When the success of the discussion is entirely in their hands, rather than the teacher's, most students rise to the challenge exceptionally well.

A different means of facilitating a free-flowing exchange of ideas is to hold online forum- or chat-based discussions. Instant messenger programs allow sessions of these text-based conversations between participants to be saved for later consideration and assessment. Alternatively, setting up a discussion forum on a webpage or Moodle server also preserves a record of the participation of each student in the discussion. In these discussions students read each other's posts and text comments, and then post their own in response. Each participant is able to see the posts of all other participants and type their own responses. When a chat system is used responses can be expected to be swift and less fully developed. When a forum is used and sufficient time given for a discussion, ranging from several hours to several days, responses can be expected to be more developed and more thoroughly supported. As noted in the previous chapter, a recent study concluded that both face-to-face and online discussion methods fulfill important but somewhat different learning objectives and should be employed accordingly. Face-to-face discussions may produce superior brainstorming, identification of important ideas, and clarifying of questions and arguments, and online text discussions may foster clearer use of explicit evidence and supportive reasoning. The aspects fostered by both methods are important to any good academic discussion. There are several ways to combine the benefits. One is to have students hold preliminary informal, small group conversations face-to-face to prepare for a subsequent more formal forum/chat-based discussion.

Grading these discussions requires reviewing the video, listening to the audio, or reading the transcripts and assessing the extent to which each student's comments meets the criteria established for the discussion. Table 5.8 suggests some criteria.

The concept and argument category will vary the most depending on the prompts given. The main goal, in any case, is to establish criteria that encourage students to develop strong insightful arguments in answer to the questions posed.

Table 5.8 **Some suggested rubric categories for a graded discussion**

Category	Standards
Concept and argument	• Student demonstrates a clear understanding of the core issues and subtleties of the prompt. • Student offers clearly articulated and supported opinions on the main questions. Conclusions go beyond the apparent. • Where there are discrepancies between the simulation and other historical source materials, the student demonstrates a clear understanding of the core and subtleties of the agreements and disagreements between the sources. • Student demonstrates a clear understanding of how the simulation functions and is able to hypothesize what the simulations suggests about the past.
Support and reasoning	• All student's main assertions, particularly those integral to their main arguments, are supported by clearly stated reasons. • Arguments are not regularly based on "common sense," i.e. unsupported belief statements, but frequently draw from a wide variety of sources that are explicitly identified and used to directly support arguments. • Discussion of a simulation is based on clear statements of observation from the simulation. • Student's inferences are compelling; student explains thoroughly and convincingly how the evidence they offer supports their point.
Process and participation	• Student engages others in the discussion by inviting their comments and acknowledging their contributions positively. • Student initiates some topics of discussion and also allows others to do so. • Student directly links their own comments to those of others by responding directly to statements made by others and/or thoughtfully challenging their accuracy, clarity, relevance or logic. • Student is a main contributor but does not dominate or monopolize the time of the discussion.

Twenty-first-century Analytical Writing: The Webpage Analysis

When it comes to authentic assessments that incorporate expository writing but also include visual and creative elements, an excellent task is to design a webpage or formal illustrated blog entry critiquing a particular game. The goals of the webpage analysis are fundamentally those of the analytical paper or discussion: research, analyze, and criticize in lucid, organized, and compelling ways. Yet the webpage paradigm offers students the chance to develop a product that has greater relevance to their lives than some assignments. In their daily lives students encounter many more webpages of all kinds and qualities than they do short expository papers. It is reasonable to suppose that many will, at some point in their professional or personal lives, design and write blogs and perhaps even webpages of their own—more than will likely write five-page formal expository essays outside of their scholastic lives.

Well structured webpages designed to convey information or opinions follow rules of effective visual design, incorporate graphics effectively to convey and enhance meaning, and also include brief but powerful and focused segments of text. There are three core elements that should be incorporated, at the very least, in a web analysis:

- Identifying game principles: This is the part where students simply reflect on what the game suggests about history. The emphasis here is not on critiquing the game, but on understanding the presentation of the game.
- Analyzing strengths: This is a criticism exercise. Students use valid research to support the basic validity of one or two of the game's models.
- Analyzing weaknesses: The flip side of the coin. Students use valid research to test the basic validity of one or two of the game's models.

These features are applicable to most, if not all, historical games. In keeping with the model of a scholarly webpage, these elements are conveyed in text and image, and supported by clear citations of valid evidence.

The webpages need not be published and need not be designed with actual webpage design software. Whether to publish or not must be considered carefully. Obtain approval from your school administrators before proceeding and be sure to follow the rules of the school and community to protect the identities of students, particularly minors. If the finished products are intended to remain in the classroom, they can be designed on paper or using most any word-processing program that allows the use of pictures and simple shapes. If the goal is to actually produce webpages, many word-processing programs offer the ability to convert their documents to HTML, the language of webpages. One can also use web services like Wordpress (www.wordpress.com) or Blogger (www.blogger.com) to post such analyses. These services do not provide much control over the layout of the analysis, and templates like the ones on the following pages would be hard to achieve this way. At the same time, self-published blogs are increasingly becoming a standard for both informal and scholarly sharing of ideas on the web.

Figure 5.6 is an example of a web-analysis template used with history students. This is one of many possible layouts, provided simply as an illustration of some basic components.

Simulation Design Proposal

Though the subject could fill a book to itself, it is worth noting that the flip side of simulation play and critique, simulation design, can also be an outstanding exercise of the historian's craft. Designing a simulation that faithfully reflects a historical process requires the historian's critical skills for developing a compelling written argument: the ability to analyze and contextualize evidence, distinguish between the trivial and the essential, advance a defensible account of causation, and, in doing so, construct a plausible interpretation of the past. The beauty of a simulation design project, however, is that it requires high level thinking that is packaged in a format readily understandable and engaging to many, if not most, students: the game.

Unfortunately, there are still few, if any, computer design tools that are both sufficiently easy to learn, yet able to allow students to create sophisticated historical settings and content quickly. Design tools are available, and they are getting easier to use, but it is far beyond the time and means for a history teacher to train students in programming concepts so that they can engage in simulation design. A solution that allows students to engage their ability to synthesize and delve into developing their own game-based interpretations without the programming overhead, is a simulation design proposal. In this exercise students research and design a proposal for a simulation game. Box 5.5 provides a sample assignment for a simulation design proposal.

Table 5.9 shows the design proposal rubric.

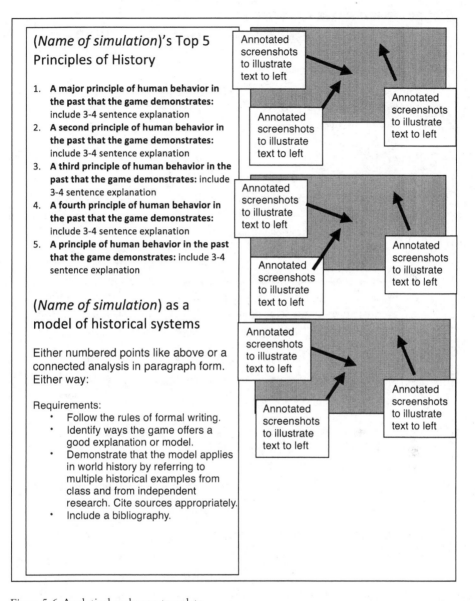

Figure 5.6 Analytical webpage template

Box 5.5 PROMPT FOR A SIMULATION DESIGN PROPOSAL

Simulation Design Proposal

Research and create a proposal for a simulation game. This proposal will be based upon valid research into an important real-world issue, past or present. Pick something that you believe is important and interests you.

Structure

1   A written or recorded component that includes the following parts:

   • Introduction—introduce the reader to your game proposal. Start with a hook to gain the reader's interest, then survey the main components of the game that will be elaborated upon in the rest of the proposal.
   • Rationale—explain both why this is an important topic for people to understand and why it is an appropriate topic for a simulation game.
   • Research overview (five valid sources minimum)—survey the historical event, processes, systems, etc. that will be treated in the game. Do not give a list of dates or other facts. Rather give a clear overview of the specific historical content the game will simulate.
   • Overview of gameplay—explain how the game looks and how it is played. Include a description of the main screens, the information the player receives, and the controls the player uses. Explain the challenges the player faces in the game and the winning and losing conditions.

2   One or more annotated mock-up screens must be created demonstrating what the game will look like and how it will be played. Include text annotation indicating what the various parts of the screen represent and do.

Complementary Writing Assignments

Developing writing skills is a paramount concern of teachers in history. The following exercises provide more opportunities to focus on writing skills. They also offer a few language arts tie-ins for integrated classrooms and for English classrooms.

Interpreting the Game's Website

Most, if not all, commercial games are supported by a website. Generally these sites tend to include an overview of the game, a list of features, and

Table 5.9 Rubric for a simulation design proposal

Category	Standards
Proposal quality, organization, and focus	• Proposal is clear, sophisticated and addresses all content areas. • Each segment of the proposal is well organized and clearly follows from the topic sentences for each paragraph. • Proposal conveys a clear sense of the importance of the topic and its suitability for treatment in a simulation game. • Historical overview is clear, well organized and focused on the elements that will be portrayed in the game. • Gameplay is described in detail and the connections between the historical content and gameplay are clearly drawn.
Support and reasoning	• Where supporting evidence is required (especially the historical overview), numerous examples of the strongest possible evidence are paraphrased or, when appropriate, quoted. • The source and context of the evidence is clear. • A legitimate citation for the evidence is given in parentheses after the evidence. • Evidence is drawn from a variety of sources. When the sources provided are limited, evidence is drawn from a wide sampling of the sources (e.g. not just one paragraph of a multi-page document).

Language, grammar and style	• Writing is grammatically and mechanically correct with the exception of a few (or no) typographical errors; Spell check has clearly been run carefully.
	• Style embodies engaging scholarly writing by:
	  – including varied, interesting, and appropriate word choices
	  – avoiding repetitive phrasing and varying sophisticated phrasing
	  – being precise and clear
	  – using transitional words and phrases effectively so that each sentence is connected to the next in an elegant fashion.

Design and style	• Proposal for gameplay is complete, offering a clear picture of how the game looks and is played. • Mockups are clear and polished offering a clear picture of how the game looks and is played.

press excerpts (when positive ones are available). In short, they provide an excellent insight into the game creators' views of their game and its strengths. Any marketing team worth its salt will include those press statements that sell the game, avoid statements that hurt the game, and accentuate those game features they think will appeal to the widest range of consumers. Studying and reporting on the website presentation of the game, therefore, is a good exercise in reading and writing about a biased source. Questions of commission and omission, presentation, phrasing, and a host of other issues come into play.

Game Reviews

A large number of print and Internet resources are devoted to reviewing computer games. Among others, major websites devoted to reviewing PC games include PC Gamer, Gamespot, Gamespy PC, IGN.com PC, and 1UP.com. Reading and summarizing one or more of these sites' reviews helps develop reading comprehension and writing skills. Many of these sites, and others as well, allow viewers to post their own reviews or at least comment on the professional reviews; indeed many gamers consider it an inalienable right to be able to post their own views. Writing an effective review, however, requires much more than just having an opinion and an Internet connection. Effective reviews summarize and describe the work in question, provide clear categories and criteria for evaluation, and judge the work according to those criteria. Having students review the reviews is an excellent twenty-first-century literacy exercise, practice in discerning valid from invalid comments. Better still, students can be charged both with critiquing existing reviews and posting their own review online—a review of the game as a historical simulation.

PUTTING TOGETHER A LESSON OR UNIT PLAN

Determining Time Requirements

Except for situations where an instructor runs a single instance of a game for the whole class, projected onto a screen, students will be players, and time demands for lessons increase. The amount of time to devote to playing and observing a game depends upon both the scope of the game and the amount of time available for playing the game. There are no hard and fast rules but rather a set of factors that will need to be balanced. At the shortest end, some games can be played in 15–20 minutes and are suitable for short homework assignments—so long as the students have access to computers and copies of the game outside of class. Most web-based games fall into this category. Most commercial games, however, require far more time to learn and play. The tutorials in most complex commercial strategy games can take anywhere from 20 minutes to 1 hour to complete. Gaining familiarity with the game can take several hours of play, depending on the student, the complexity of the game, and the elements of the game the teacher wants students to experience. Table 5.10 provides some estimates for time requirements.

A couple of notes are relevant here. First, the actual time requirements for a game will vary depending on the facility with which students learn

Table 5.10 **Estimated times for learning and playing various kinds of simulation games**

Time	Game types	Examples
15–45 minutes	Most browser-based games	*Who Wants to be a Cotton Millionaire* (BBC) *Third World Farmer* Chevron's *Energyville* *Muck and Brass* (BBC).
45 minutes–1.5 hours	The tutorial or training session in a demo commercial game; an easily learned but longer browser-based game.	*Real Lives 2010* *Total War* demos *Stronghold 2 demo* *Ayiti* *Climate Challenge.*
1.5–3 hours	The tutorial or training session and adequate gameplay for a game of moderate complexity. Many demos fit in this category.	A scenario in a shorter commercial simulation (*Political Machine*) Multiple historical battles in any of the *Total War* games Most city-builder games Simple war games Demos.
4+ hours	The tutorial or training session and experiencing in some depth a commercial game of moderate complexity	*City-builders* *Civilization* (not a complete game) Campaign mode in the *Total War* games and most other war games.
6+ hours (could extend to 10+)	The tutorial or training session and extensive play of longer campaign games	*City-builders* *Civilization* (a complete game depending on settings and the speed of the player) Campaign mode in the *Total War* games Nation-building games.

to play the game and the level of familiarity with a game the teacher wishes them to acquire. Second, these times are not meant to indicate time that must be taken solely from the classroom. Any appropriate game with an adequate tutorial can be played mostly or completely outside of class so long as the necessary resources are available—an open computer lab, or the ability for students to play at home. If resources for play outside class are not available, however, be sure to budget enough time for gameplay in class. Too little, and the exercise loses its educational value.

Finally, it is important to distinguish between the time needed to learn a game and the time needed to play and observe a game. Learning to play a complex game requires consistent time and practice at the beginning. Once the game has been learned, one can play less frequently. What this means in practice is that scheduling several homework/class periods of gameplay close together when first learning the game is extremely helpful. Once the game has been learned, it is possible to spread out gameplay assignments so that students are playing once every week or two. So, for example, a class might spend several hours in the first week initially learning to play a complex game like *Civilization*, then reduce play time to 30 minutes every other week or so throughout the term. This sort of arrangement works well when using a game throughout a longer unit of study

General Lesson and Unit Formats

The general components of lessons involving game-based simulations was set out in the previous chapter. Students need to learn to play, gain solid play experience, observe and analyze the game in action, and have time to reflect and debrief. When the purpose is to have students engage with and reflect upon the games without reference to any particular evidence sets, this standard structure will serve and teachers can use the table above as a rough guideline for time needed to learn to play and play. A two-day lesson outline that includes training in gameplay could look like as shown in Table 5.11.

This plan could be adapted in a variety of ways, including an addition of one or more days for gameplay. A brief debriefing discussion on the third day of class is also an effective extension choice. Additionally, instead of written reflections, analysis exercises selected from the options in this chapter can be substituted.

A three-day plan that begins with a class analysis of evidence relevant to critiquing the simulation is modeled in Table 5.12, using the simulation *Ayiti*; this will work with any reasonably short game.

Among a number of other possible adaptations for a three-day plan, evidence can be assigned to students to read and examine as homework prior to the classes, and any of the exercises contained in this chapter can be used instead of reflective writings. As the time devoted to the game increases, so do opportunities to conduct more analytical exercises and produce more varied assessments based on the simulation. The sample five-day plan shown in Table 5.13 suggests just one possibility.

These templates offer only a few of the large number of possible plans. Again, the critical point is that simulation game-based lessons, whether spanning a day or a week, should incorporate:

Table 5.11 Template for two-day lesson

Day	Learning outcomes	Instructional strategies/ activities	Assessment
1	Students will: • Learn to play the simulation. • Complete a set of notes on a play guide for the game.	• Introduce the purpose of the simulation exercise. • Direct instruction of gameplay. Students follow along and take notes to create (or add to) a play guide. • Teacher explains a set of game objectives for the next class.	Written homework: Describe how to play the simulation game based on class instruction.
2	Students will: • Learn to play the simulation. • Analyze the simulation in terms of the key challenges and trade-offs presented. • Raise questions about the accuracy of the simulation.	• Teacher reminds students about the objectives for the play session. • Students play individually or in pairs. • At end of class, students complete an observation sheet for the game.	Homework: • Completed observation sheets. • Written reflection: "What are the key challenges that you face in the simulation game world?" • Write down at least two questions about how the real world works raised by the game.

Table 5.12 Template for three-day lesson based on *Ayiti*

Day	Learning outcomes	Instructional strategies/ activities	Assessment
1	Students will: • Comprehend and be able to apply the standards for global poverty to Haiti. • Comprehend critical statistics for the state of global poverty. • Analyze and synthesize data in order to build a picture of the state of poverty in Haiti.	• Teacher provides direct instruction overview of Haiti. • Small-group analysis of statistics and documents (personal testimonies from people in poverty and aid workers?) relevant to global poverty. • Each group crafts written reflection and makes oral presentation.	Written reflection: "Based on the evidence what are the challenges that families struggling with poverty in developing nations face?"

continued . . .

Table 5.12 continued . . .

Day	Learning outcomes	Instructional strategies/activities	Assessment
2	Students will: • Learn to play the simulation *Ayiti*. • Analyze the simulation in terms of the key challenges and trade-offs those without resources face in Haiti. Attempt to empathize with those who face difficult choices. • Raise questions about the accuracy of the simulation.	• Teacher introduces simulations as a tool for studying systems. • Teacher introduces the game and core gameplay through direct instruction. • Students play in pairs and complete an observation sheet. • Class discussion.	• Completed observation sheets. • Class discussion. • Homework: reflection: "What are the key challenges that faced your family in *Ayiti*?" • Write down at least two questions about how the real world works raised by the game.
3	Students will: • Assess the accuracy of the simulation using the evidence they have surveyed. • Craft a proposal to help alleviate poverty in Haiti.	• Introduce the criterion for a valid simulation and the approach to critiquing a simulation. • Class meets in small groups to discuss the validity of the simulation using reference to the evidence from day 1. • Whole class discussion.	• Critical essay on the accuracy of *Ayiti* as a simulation. • Web-ad promoting a strategy for alleviating poverty in Haiti.

Table 5.13 Template for a five-day unit

Day	Learning outcomes	Instructional strategies/activities	Assessment
1	Students will: • Learn to play the simulation. • Analyze the simulation in terms of the inherent challenges and trade-offs.	• Teacher introduces the game and core gameplay through direct instruction. • Students begin to work toward a set of game goals set by the teacher. Progress is saved at the end of class.	Homework: • First reflection on gameplay. • Write down at least two questions about how the real world works raised by the game.

continued . . .

Table 5.13 continued ...

Day	Learning outcomes	Instructional strategies/ activities	Assessment
2	Students will: • Continue to learn to play the simulation. • Begin making observation notes. • Analyze the simulation in terms of the inherent challenges and trade-offs.	• Teacher introduces observation sheets to students. • Students continue to work toward a set of game goals set by teacher. • Teacher circulates around the room helping students as needed. • Students are instructed to pause play every 10 minutes and take observation notes for 3 minutes.	Homework: • Second reflection on gameplay. • Write down at least two more questions about how the real world works raised by the game.
3	Students will: • Devise observational strategies for observing simulation models. • Observe the simulation and take notes on the results. • Analyze the models in the simulation.	• Teacher present students with a set of analytical questions about the game. • Brainstorm methods for answering the questions through game analysis. • Students work in pairs to answer each of the questions following the methods set in class.	Homework: • Draw a set of diagrams illustrating the game models studied in class.
4	Students will: • Evaluate the strengths and weaknesses of the simulation.	• Teacher introduce the criteria for a valid simulation and the approach to critiquing a simulation. • Informal class discussion on validity of the simulation using reference to the evidence sets read as homework.	Design a webpage analysis and critique of the game.
5	Summative assessment	• Formal online, forum-based discussion of the strengths and weaknesses of the simulation game.	Online discussion

- An introduction to the purposes of the simulation exercise of greater or lesser detail depending on students' familiarity with using simulation games.
- Opportunity before or after simulation play, when possible and practical, for students to study independent evidence relevant to the simulation, discuss it, and form some initial conclusions about the historical topic of study.
- Time and the necessary support to learn how to play the game. Explicit opportunities to observe and make notes on the game.
- Frequent opportunities to analyze and reflect upon the game using any of the various exercises covered in this and the last chapter.
- Some form of collective final reflection and debriefing.

These are the hallmarks of powerful, effective lessons using simulation games.

FINAL THOUGHTS

Several years ago, James Gee explored the idea of models in education and suggested:

> It may well be that when educators recruit games for learning in areas like science or social science the role of models and modeling will be a critical aspect. The fact that video games can give players rich experiences, allow them to interpret and reflect on these experiences, and, at the same time, get them to interact with models at various levels of abstraction as part and parcel of those experiences . . . may eventually be seen as one of the promising aspects of games in learning.
>
> (Gee, 2007: 164)

That his prediction will prove accurate is likely, but it will take teachers in the classroom implementing and refining instructional strategies to bring this recognition about. To that end, this book has served as a point of departure, an initial compilation of different facets of simulation game use that will provide educators with enough ideas and tools to introduce games to their classrooms.

Before closing, however, it is worth considering why some teachers may feel uncomfortable, if not outright skeptical, at the prospect of using simulations as learning tools. For some this may be due to the pressures of standardized curricula. Educators teaching in such situations may feel that there is little room to innovate, to deviate from traditional methods of instruction and the prescribed curriculum. There are ways, however, for teachers with less flexible curricula to incorporate simulation games effectively in the classroom. As we have seen there are simulations of all lengths and levels of complexity addressing a wide variety of topics and periods. There are commercial simulation games and a host of freely available web-based simulations. Using a simulation game does not necessarily require that teachers spend days away from the other elements in their curriculum. More importantly, the variety of simulations and the varieties of ways students can learn with simulations mean that time spent with simulations can be wholly integrated with other learning objectives and methods.

Learning, as is well known, is a far more complicated matter than the simple transmission of information from teacher to student. In this light the real questions are what do students learn if their teachers refuse to innovate, stretch, and adapt to a changing world; what do students learn about lifelong learning if their teachers insist only on using traditional methods of instruction? In a multimedia, rapidly changing world that defies easy prescriptions and predictions, can students be prepared for twenty-first-century demands if they learn that teachers are the sole source of authority and knowledge; that only traditional methods of learning are useful; that interpretations of the world, especially historical interpretations, can only be received and critiqued in speech and text, never in image and code? Part of the response to such questions are simulation games; they can play an integral role for students learning the twenty-first-century discipline of history as one means of equipping themselves for the future.

This instructional tool certainly does require that teachers have some confidence and skill in the discipline of history. When class shifts from focusing on the interpretations of experts to engaging with open-ended modeling, interpretation, and evidence-based critique, the teacher must go from being the sole source of knowledge to an expert guide. There will be times when the teacher simply does not have a solution to the questions students will raise in this environment. This is precisely as it should be if the goal is to inculcate in students the ability to function as independent critical thinkers rather than simply rely upon the most convenient or most attractive source of authority for answers and interpretations. Adopting the principles embedded in this model of simulation-based study can help transform history classes into something that more closely approximates the inquiries of the professionals in the discipline. It is a critical time to make the change. There are so many competing claims to the truth instantly accessible in the world today. A variety of vocal, videogenic, and/or web-centric pundits, preachers, politicians, and pop stars offer versions of reality that are often in conflict and in need of critique. Educated people, which it is our primary goal to help students set out to be, must be able to judge the validity not only of discrete facts, but of competing claims about the world of the past, present, and future. Students who learn to do history as a twenty-first-century discipline that involves a vast array of media and models have the opportunity to acquire crucial skills of critique, analysis and interpretation of human events. By learning that interpretations are not only captured in writing, but are embedded in podcasts, video mash-ups, and, of course, video games, students will acquire important skills and insights for navigating the world.

Profiles of Historical Video Games

This appendix profiles many of the commercial and non-profit games available for PCs running Windows XP, Vista, and 7—and Macintoshes (though far fewer are available for Macs). The profiles are current as of November 2010; all commercial games listed are currently available through online vendors and many through retail stores. Likewise, the URLs for web-based games are accurate at the time of publication, but if a link no longer works, try finding the game using a search engine. Fortunately, the rise of online digital distribution of software has made it increasingly likely that most, if not all, of the commercial games listed below will continue to be made available for the foreseeable future. As new games are published, look to historicalsimulation.org for updates.

New games will be created that are not covered by these profiles, however. When considering a new game the best method for learning about it is to play it. Otherwise there are a number of resources available to learn about new games and keep informed about games in general. Many organizations offer excellent online reviews of video games. The best of these are professionally run, and, though some of the reviews on some sites can sometimes be written by amateurs, the overall quality is maintained by the organization. The standard places are:

- PC Gamer—www.pcgamer.com
- 1UP—www.1up.com
- Gamespot—www.gamespot.com
- IGN—www.ign.com
- GamesRadar—www.gamesradar.com

With the exception of PC Gamer, each of these sites deals with all the major gaming platforms, not just PCs, so it is important to make sure any particular review is of the PC version of the game—not for, say, Xbox or Playstation. Reviews should be taken with a grain of salt, and it is always a good idea to review a game personally before using it in the class. These reviews are written for an audience of gamers and they are intended to assess games from an entertainment perspective. A game that did not receive a high rating from the perspective of pure entertainment may still be an excellent option for a classroom simulation.

Special mention should be made of *PC Gamer* magazine, which is published in both U.S. and U.K. editions. This is one of the only major print publications in English focused solely on PC gaming. It is an outstanding monthly magazine full of previews of games to come and reviews of current games. A subscription to this magazine is well worth it for anyone wanting to keep current with PC gaming.

Being aware of genres and sequels can help greatly when reviewing unknown games. Though games can and do come along with innovative gameplay, most fit solidly within existing genres. If a game promotes itself as a city-builder, therefore, one can be reasonably certain that the core gameplay will be similar in flavor to the city-builders reviewed here. Sequels of successful games will often, though not always, continue the successful elements of their predecessors. *Civilization*, *Total War*, and the nation-building games published by Paradox Entertainment, to name just a few examples, tend to be very consistent in their look and feel with previous entries in their respective series.

Whenever possible look for games with free demo versions that can be tested before use in a class. Demos for new games are scattered across the Internet, and it is often simplest just to enter the name of the game and "demo" into a search engine. Several sites and services systematically provide demos as part of their normal operations. Steam, the leading digital distribution service of games, has a regular complement of demos to offer. One has to download the Steam client to use the service, but the client, browsing, and demos are free—users only have to pay when they purchase a commercial game.

GUIDE TO PROFILES

The profiles in this chapter are divided chronologically into historical periods and, where there are sufficient games in a period, listed alphabetically by sub-topics. Browser-based games for a historical period are listed together at the end of the period. Profiling every game available is unfeasible at best. New games continue to be issued as this book goes to print, and existing games continue to come to light that never received much in the way of press and recognition. Nor would I claim to be familiar with every historical simulation game available. To provide as much current information as possible to teachers and not exclude potentially excellent games that are less familiar, there are "Other Possibilities" listings at the end of some subtopics and historical periods. These entries are limited to a brief description in addition to the standard game information provided for each entry.

The standard profile entry has the following categories. The title and a series of tags start the entry as outlined here:

> *Title*
> *Genre; Mac version available; browser-based; demo (if demo available); multiplayer (if the game has multiplayer options); publisher/developer's website; $ (if game is not free); current direct link to official game site (if available)*

There are a few important things to note about the tags:

- All games profiled run on PC so there is no tag for PC only.
- All games profiled are single player games, so the multiplayer tags mean the game includes a multiplayer option, not that the game is a multiplayer game.

Following the title and tags are a set of categories:

Overview: A brief description of the game.

Challenge/Play Time: An assessment of the complexity of gameplay and the amount of time needed to experience the game meaningfully. Both are estimates based on a hypothetical player aged 12–20; these are, of course, estimates only. A game's challenge level is rated low, moderate, or high based on the effort needed to learn to play and acclimate to the game; *the challenge of winning the game is not estimated.* Low challenge games are more easily played and will generally require less formal training to play. Games of moderate challenge should be approached using the guidelines for training and acclimation addressed in Chapter 4. High challenge games are playable and often excellent simulations, but will require extra time to learn. Consider placing students in teams and conducting the simulation over a longer period to help ease students into high challenge games. Play time has four levels, estimates of the minimum amount of time needed for students to learn to play and acclimate to the game, not necessarily to complete the game. These levels correspond essentially to the times provided in Table 5.10. Quick games can be played in anywhere from fifteen minutes to one hour. Short games will take somewhere between one and two hours to play. Medium length games will take three to six hours. Long games may take six or more hours. Again, these are estimates of the necessary time to acclimate and observe the game; one can easily spend more time on any but the shortest and simplest of games.

Topics: A list of historical topics addressed by the games to aid in planning. To aid U.S. high school teachers who need their lessons to conform to state and national content standards in social studies, a list of voluntary U.S. national standards in World History, U.S. History, Geography, and Economics that are addressed by the games follows the topics in parentheses. The numbering of the standards matches that found on the relevant organizations' websites, specifically:

- World History (WH)—National Center for History in the Schools nchs.ucla.edu/standards/world-standards5–12.html
- U.S. History (US)—National Center for History in the Schools nchs.ucla.edu/standards/us-standards5–12.html
- Geography (G)—U.S. National Geography Standards www.nationalgeographic.com/xpeditions/standards/matrix.html
- Economics (EC)—Council for Economic Education EconomicsAmerica® Standards www.councilforeconed.org/ea/standards

GAME LISTINGS

ANCIENT WORLD—EGYPTIANS

Immortal Cities: Children of the Nile (2004)

City-building; demo; Tilted Mill (www.tiltedmill.com); $ www.immortalcities.com/cotn/

Overview: Develop and rule an Egyptian settlement along the Nile. Though *CotN* focuses on an Egyptian setting, it is a standard city-builder requiring the player to construct buildings, manage food supplies, and see to the needs of the populace. One strength of the game is the representation of the link between seasons and agriculture, a connection generally ignored by other games.

Challenge/Play Time: Moderate challenge/Medium length. *CotN* is a bit more difficult to learn than some city-builders, simply because the game controls are less polished. The tutorial, however, is effective at teaching players.

Topics: Financial management and economic development; Egyptian architecture; urban geography, urban planning, and urban systems; elements of daily life in Egypt; trade; basic Egyptian physical geography. (WH 2.1–2; G 12, 14, 15; EC 1, 2, 3, 4, 15)

Other Possibilities

History Egypt: Engineering an Empire (2010)

Turn-based nation-building, city-building, and war; multiplayer; Slitherine (www.slitherine.com); $
The player rules a part of Egypt and attempts to establish an empire through sound economic, political, military, and diplomatic policies. The game combines elements of turn-based city-building, nation-building, and simplified strategic and tactical combat.

ANCIENT WORLD—ROMANS

Roman City-builders

Caesar IV (2006)

City-building; demo; multiplayer; Tilted Mill (www.tiltedmill.com); $
Overview: In *Caesar IV* the player places public and private buildings, roads, and water supplies, while the inhabitants of the city travel to work and satisfy their needs. The main outlines of the game are similar to *CivCity: Rome*, though *Caesar* has a different feel from *CivCity*. The daisy chain economy is not as pronounced. In addition, property values are heavily influenced by neighboring properties—so access to a butcher is important but living next to a butcher will limit a house's property value.
Challenge/Play Time: Moderate challenge/Medium length
Topics: See *CivCity: Rome*

CivCity: Rome (2006)

City-building; 2K Games (www.2kgames.com); $
www.2kgames.com/civcityrome/civcity.html
Overview: Build a Roman city from the ground up. Manage food supplies and handle the economic, security, and entertainment needs of citizens in an attempt to make the city prosper.

Challenge/Play Time: Moderate challenge/Medium length. The tutorial is good, though providing formal in-class training can be very helpful. Some of the missions in the campaign mode are quite challenging. The player is given plenty of money on the easiest game setting, however, to offset the challenge.

Topics: Financial management and economic development; Roman architecture; urban geography, urban planning, and urban systems; elements of daily life in Roman cities; trade; basic Mediterranean geography. (WH 3.5, 4.1; G 12, 14, 15; EC 1, 2, 3, 4, 15)

Glory of the Roman Empire (2009)

City-building; demo; Kalypso Media (www.kalypsomedia.com/en-us); $ www.grandages.com

Overview: Another Roman city-builder, gameplay in *GRE* is similar to *CivCity: Rome* and *Caesar IV*. Unlike these games, however, *GRE* represents the time and resources involved in construction. When a site for a building is designated, scaffolding appears. The final building is completed over time and only so long as sufficient building materials are available. *GRE* also lacks the anachronistic research component of *CivCity: Rome*. The buildings and landscapes are excellently rendered and large scale settlements can be built and managed.

Challenge/Play Time: Moderate challenge/Medium length

Topics: See *CivCity: Rome*

Imperium Romanum (2008) and Grand Ages: Rome (2009)

City-building; demo; Kalypso Media (www.kalypsomedia.com/en-us/); $ www.grandages.com/us/iromanum.php

Overview: *Imperium Romanum* and *Grand Ages: Rome* are both sequels to *Glory of the Roman Empire*. Both have the same city-building mechanic as their predecessor with updated graphics. In addition players must now defend their cities from computer rivals' attacks and can besiege enemy cities. These battles are highly stylized, however, and not a serious point of accuracy in the simulations. Those interested in ancient battle are far better served by *Rome: Total War*.

Challenge/Play Time: Moderate challenge/Medium length

Topics: See *CivCity: Rome*

Roman War and Imperialism

Europa Universalis: Rome

Real-time nation-building; Mac version available; demo; multiplayer; Paradox Entertainment (www.paradoxplaza.com); $ www.paradoxplaza.com/rome/

Overview: *EU: Rome* is a modified version of the standard *Europa Universalis* game, designed to allow players to lead the Roman Republic, Empire, or one of a number of other historical factions. Similar to *EU 3*, all strategic play takes play on a map, in this case of the Mediterranean. The map is divided into distinct political territories but also can be viewed topographically. The player manages the Romans' economy, trade, diplomacy, and military at the strategic level. As with *EU3*, *EU: Rome* takes considerable time to learn to play effectively but is packed with historical detail.

Challenge/Play Time: High challenge/Long; the tutorials are detailed and helpful, but expect to put significant time and effort into learning how to play.

Topics: Financial management and economic development; trade; basic Mediterranean physical geography; political geography of third-century BCE Mediterranean; ancient Mediterranean political, economic, and military systems; diplomacy. (WH 3.2, 3.3, 4.1; G 4, 8, 12, 13, 15; EC 1, 2, 5)

Rome: Total War (2004)

Turn-based nation-building and campaign/real-time strategy; Mac version available; demo; multiplayer; Creative Assembly (www.creative-assembly.co.uk/); $ www.totalwar.com

Overview: Play the role of a Roman family faction leader out to acquire an empire. Conduct turn-based diplomacy, nation-building, and grand military strategies on a stylized topographical map of the Mediterranean. Wage tactical battles in real-time between units of ancient infantry, cavalry, and missile troops.

Challenge/Play Time: Moderate challenge/Short length for an individual battle; Medium length for part of a campaign. Playing the demo or any individual battle is easier than playing the campaign.

Topics: Roman and other ancient types of infantry, cavalry, and artillery; equipment and weapons; physical geography of the Mediterranean;

political powers of ancient Mediterranean; features of Roman cities. (WH 3.5, 4.1; G 4, 8, 12, 13, 15; EC 1, 2, 5)

Other Possibilities—Roman Warfare

Field of Glory and Field of Glory—Rise of Rome Expansion

Turn-based war; multiplayer; Slitherine (www.slitherine.com); $

Field of Glory is a turn-based adaptation of a miniature war game about ancient warfare. Accordingly, units are represented as handfuls of figures reminiscent of tabletop miniatures, and the map is divided into hexagonal spaces. The *Rise of Rome* expansion adds a number of Roman armies to the original game.

History Channel Great Battles of Rome

Real-time war; Slitherine (www.slitherine.com); $

Command Roman armies in real-time tactical battles punctuated by excerpts from History Channel documentaries. Battles are conducted in *RTW* style, though troops are more generic and gameplay less sophisticated. There is no campaign aspect to the game.

Browser-Based Games

Battlefield Academy

Turn-based war; browser-based; BBC (www.bbc.co.uk/history/interactive/games/)

In this simple turn-based war-game players must win four battles representative of different periods of warfare: Roman, medieval, Napoleonic, and Second World War. Each battlefield is represented by a simplified, top-down map of terrain divided into squares. Units are similarly represented by simple figures viewed top-down, and the player commands these units to move and attack through mouse clicks. The designers assert that the computer opponent adapts to the player's strategies as the battle progresses. Finally, the help section focuses on the key skills generals need to win battles and provides some basic content.

Emperor of Rome Game

Scripted decision-making; browser-based; PBS (www.pbs.org) www.pbs.org/empires/romans/special/ emperor_game.html

In the role of Augustus, Claudius, or Nero, the player is presented with a series of dilemmas described in text and accompanied by supporting visuals. For each dilemma the player may select one of three or four options. An assessment of the success of the choice follows, including a survey of what the real emperor actually did. Then the player is presented with the next dilemma. At the end an overall assessment of the player/emperor's reign is provided.

MEDIEVAL EUROPE

Political and Military

Medieval: Total War II

Turn-based nation-building and campaign/real-time strategy; demo; multiplayer; Creative Assembly (www.creative-assembly.co.uk/); $ www.totalwar.com

Overview: Another installment in the *Total War* series, *Medieval: Total War II* puts the player in the role of a medieval ruler. Diplomacy and trade components have been polished, making *MTW*'s campaign a bit more sophisticated than *RTW*'s. The Papacy is now a player in international relations, adding to the complexity of politics. The campaign includes economically and militarily distinct castles and towns. The battle simulator treats medieval warfare comparably to how *RTW* represents ancient battles and does so with a more sophisticated graphics engine that allows individual soldiers to be armed and clothed differently from their comrades in the same unit.

Challenge/Play Time: Moderate challenge/Short length for an individual battle; Medium length for a partial campaign. Playing the demo or any individual battle is easier than playing the campaign.

Topics: Medieval European, North African, and West Asian types of infantry, cavalry, and artillery; equipment and weapons; physical geography of the Mediterranean and Europe; political powers of medieval Europe, North Africa, and West Asia; features of wooden and stone medieval castles and towns; trade goods, basic diplomacy, the Catholic Church as a political power. (WH 4.1, 4.4, 5.2, 6.4; G 4, 8, 12, 13, 15; EC 1, 2, 5)

Other Possibilities—Medieval Political and Military

XIII Century

Real-time war; multiplayer; Aspyr (www.aspyr.com); $ http://xiiicentury.1cpublishing.eu/

Command medieval armies in real-time tactical battles on realistic terrain. *XIII Century*'s model for real-time tactical battles is comparable, though not as polished as that of *Medieval: Total War*. The game does incorporate a greater emphasis on Central and Eastern European warfare than *MTW*.

Great Invasions

Turn-based military, nation-building, and military strategy; multiplayer; Ageod (www.ageod.com); $

A simulation of politics, economics, diplomacy, and war in the early Middle Ages, c. 375–1066. Depending on the period selected (the three stages of the game cover 375–632, 632–843, and 843–1066), command the armies of the late Roman Empire, Germanic tribes, Islamic Empire, Viking Kingdoms, Byzantine Empire, and the Carolingian Franks.

History Great Battles Medieval

Real-time tactical battles; Slitherine (www.slitherine.com); $

Command armies from the Hundred Years War in real-time tactical battles punctuated by excerpts from History Channel documentaries. Like the developer's comparable title, *Great Battle Rome*, this game offers a more generic model of medieval warfare than *Medieval: Total War*.

Lionheart: King's Crusade

Real-time war; demo; Paradox Interactive (www.paradoxplaza.com); $ www.lionheartthegame.com

Overview: Lead a crusade as Richard the Lionheart or rally the defense against the Christian invaders as Saladin. *Lionheart* uses a tactical battle system similar to that found in the *Total War* series. The campaign requires players to use a strategic map to plan and fight battles at key locations in the medieval Holy Land. As Richard, the player must also balance the demands of various crusading factions (the Templars, French, Holy Roman Emperors, and Papacy). Access to different types of support depends on the player's ability to manage these factions.

Montjoie!

Turn-based diplomacy and military strategy; multiplayer; Ageod (www.ageod.com); $

Montjoie! is a computer version of a successful turn-based tabletop game about the Hundred Years War. Gameplay focuses on conducting diplomacy, raising armies, building castles, and waging war. A timeline and set of brief historical entries provide additional information about the Hundred Years War.

Manor/City-builders

Dawn of Discovery

City-building; demo; Ubisoft (www.ubi.com); $ dawnofdiscoverygame.us.ubi.com/pc/

Overview: *Dawn of Discovery* is the sequel to *1701 AD* (see entry under Early Modern Europe—Exploration and Colonization). Like its predecessor, the main focus is on building cities and managing trade routes. The setting is now late medieval Europe and Asia. A campaign mode includes the story of a fictional European crusade against the East, though the individual scenarios allow the player to skip this element.

Challenge/Play Time: Moderate challenge/Medium length

Topics: Financial management and economic development; late medieval European urban architecture; urban geography, urban planning, and urban systems; elements of daily life; trade; production of goods. (WH 5.5, 6.1; G 12, 14, 15; EC 1, 2, 3, 5, 15)

Stronghold 2 (2005)

City-building, real-time siege warfare; demo; multiplayer; 2K Games (www.2kgames.com); $ www.2kgames.com/stronghold2

Overview: Players build and manage a medieval manor and castle, tending to the economic, military, agricultural, entertainment, and legal aspects of manor life. (See Chapter 3.)

Challenge/Play Time: Moderate challenge/Medium length. The tutorial that accompanies the demo is thorough.

Topics: Financial management and economic development; manorialism and geographical characteristics of manors; lord–peasant relations; castle elements; medieval manufacturing and agriculture; food and entertainment; siege warfare. (WH 4.4, 4.7, 5.2; G 12, 14, 15; EC 1, 2, 3, 4, 15)

Stronghold Crusader (2005)

City-building, real-time siege warfare; demo; multiplayer; 2K Games (www.2kgames.com); $

Overview: *Stronghold Crusader* is an earlier version of the *Stronghold 2* focused on the Crusader States. The graphical engine is less sophisticated than that of *Stronghold 2*, but the game is very similar in core gameplay.

Challenge/Play Time: See *Stronghold 2*

Topics: See *Stronghold 2*

Trade

Patrician 3

Trade and economic strategy; multiplayer; Ascaron (www.ascaron.com); $

Overview: An intensive, detail-oriented, economic simulation of Hanseatic merchants trading in fifteenth-century Northern European cities. The player begins the game with a cargo ship and a sum of money. By making successful trades of cargo between various cities— buying goods at a low price and selling them for more in ports that demand the goods—the player builds a fortune. Successful players can expand their fleets and even come to dominate the economy and politics of their home city.

Challenge/Play Time: Moderate–high/Long. The tutorials are helpful and should be played.

Topics: Trade, financial management and economic development; late medieval trade routes and goods; characteristics of medieval trading cities; characteristics of late medieval ships. (WH 5.5; G 11, 16; E 1, 2, 5, 6, 15)

Other Medieval Trade Possibilities

Patrician IV

Trade and economic strategy; multiplayer; Ascaron (www.ascaron.com); $

Fundamentally similar to *Patrician III* in that the player acts as one of the Hanseatic merchants trading in fifteenth-century Europe, *Patrician IV* has an updated interface and graphics.

Browser-Based Games

Battle of Hastings

Scripted decision-making; browser-based; BBC (www.bbc.co.uk/history/interactive/games/)

In this short game, the player takes the role of William or Harold. When the game begins, the player is presented with limited set of tactical choices. The effects of the player's choice are displayed on a simplified battlefield with a handful of units representing the far greater number of historical combatants. Then the player is presented with another option, which is also played out. The game is not deep but does illustrate the basic facets of this particular battle.

Battlefield Academy

Turn-based war; browser-based; BBC (www.bbc.co.uk/history/interactive/games/)

See the description under Ancient World—Romans. The player must win the Roman battle to gain access to the medieval battle.

Viking Quest

Scripted decision-making; browser-based; BBC (www.bbc.co.uk/history/interactive/games/)

Assuming the command of a Viking raid on northern Britain, the player makes choices from a series of options about the type of boat, crew, and route to take. Once landfall is made in Britain, the player selects from a series of choices about how to attack a nearby monastery. The overall success of the player's raid is reported at the end.

Other Medieval Possibilities

The Guild 2 (2005)

Role playing, life management; demo; multiplayer;
JoWood Games (www.jowood.com); $
www.diegilde2.com
Build a family dynasty in a medieval town. Engage in trade, family rivalries, and local politics.

EARLY MODERN EUROPE/OLD REGIME

Exploration and Colonization

1701 A.D./Anno 1701 (2006)

City-building; demo; multiplayer; Aspyr
(www.aspyr.com); $
Overview: *1701 AD* applies the city-builder genre to the topic of European colonial settlements. The player must plant and develop a generically Anglo-European style colony in a new land, trade with other colonies, and deliver raw materials back to the mother country. As the colony evolves, the demands of the settlers grow increasingly expensive to fulfill.

Challenge/Play Time: Moderate/Medium. The game itself is equivalent in its difficulty to any other city-builder. The tutorial, however, is easily one of the most thorough around, not only telling players what to build and why, but where to build.

Topics: Financial management and economic development; early modern European urban architecture; urban geography, urban planning, and urban systems; elements of daily life in colonial settlements; trade; production of goods; motives for colonization. (US 1.2, 2.1, 2.3; WH 6.1, 6.6; G 12, 14, 15; EC 1, 2, 3, 5, 15)

Civilization IV: Colonization, FreeCol

Turn-based strategy; Mac version available; Firaxis
(www.firaxis.com); $ (except FreeCol)
FreeCol: www.freecol.org
Overview: Colonize a new world. Found settlements, establish peaceful or hostile relations with natives, and develop an economy producing

raw materials and trading them with the mother country. Unlike *1701*, *Colonization* focuses on the building of an entire colonial presence up to and including inevitable revolution from the European mother country. The game is a modified version of *Civilization IV* and gameplay is similar.

Challenge/Play Time: Moderate/Medium–long

Topics: Financial management and economic development; elements of daily life in colonial settlements; trade; production of goods; motives for colonization; impact of colonization on indigenous peoples; relationship between colonies and home governments. (US 2.1, 2.2, 2.3; WH 6.2, 6.4; G 4, 8, 11, 12, 13, 15; E 1, 2, 3, 5, 6, 15)

Other Possibilities—Exploration and Colonization

Commander: Conquest of the Americas

Trade and economic strategy, naval battles; demo;
Paradox Interactive (www.paradoxplaza.com); $
www.cota-game.com

As the head of one of several European nations, the player plants a colony and develops an economic empire trading commodities and goods between Europe and the Americas. Play is similar to *East India Company* in the focus on trade and, when necessary, naval combat with rivals.

Nation-building

Europa Universalis 3

Real-time nation-building; Mac version available; demo;
Paradox Interactive (www.paradoxplaza.com); $
www.europauniversalis3.com

Overview: Rule any nation in the world from the period 1415–1789 in this epic simulation game of political and military management. Play takes place on a map of the world divided into provinces that can be viewed through a political filter or topographically. Research technologies, political and social philosophies; manage finances and trade; develop provinces; recruit armies; engage in detailed foreign policy; and conduct wars. This is the most comprehensive nation-building simulation for the period available, though it will take time and commitment to learn to play.

Challenge/Play Time: High/Long; the tutorials are detailed and helpful, but expect to put significant time into learning how to play.

Topics: Early modern political, economic, and military systems; diplomacy, world physical geography and fifteenth–nineteenth-century political geography; financial management and economic development. (US 1.2; 2.1 WH 6.3, 6.4, 7.3; G 4, 8, 12, 13, 15; EC 1, 2, 5)

Trade

East India Company

Trade and economic strategy, naval battles; demo;
Paradox Interactive (www.paradoxplaza.com); $
www.eic-game.com/

Overview: As the head of one of several European nations' East India Companies, the player develops an economic empire in Southern Asia and Africa. As with many other trade simulations, the player begins with one fleet and a lump sum of money. With these resources she develops trade routes between a European home port—London, for example—and cities in Africa and Asia. Eventually the player can raise sufficient funds to hire warships and marines and secure complete control over one or more foreign ports. All the while, the player must compete with other European East India Companies similarly seeking to dominate the eastern trade routes.

Challenge/Play Time: Moderate/Medium length. The tutorials are helpful and should be played.

Topics: Trade; financial management and economic development; early modern trade routes and goods; coastal geography of Africa and India; characteristics of European trade and war ships; naval warfare. (WH 5.5; G 11, 16; E 1, 2, 5, 6, 15)

Port Royale 2

Trade and economic strategy; multiplayer; Ascaron
(www.ascaron.com); $

Overview: Port Royale is from the same designers as *Patrician III* and has fundamentally similar game mechanics. Now the player starts with a ship and a sum of money in the Caribbean. They must build an economic empire by buying low and selling high as they trade goods between the ports of the Caribbean. Prices for goods differ from port to port and change as supply and demand change. This is an excellent simulation requiring the same type of commitment as *Patrician III*.

Challenge/Play Time: Moderate–high/Long. The tutorials are helpful and should be played.

Topics: Trade; financial management and economic development; sixteenth- and seventeenth-century Caribbean geography and trade routes; piracy. (WH 6.4; G 4, 11, 12, 13; E 1, 2, 5, 6).

Sid Meier's Pirates

Real-time economic strategy/ship combat; Mac version available; Firaxis (www.firaxis.com); $ www.2kgames.com/pirates/

Overview: Take command of a small ship and lead a life of privateering in the service of Britain, France, Holland, or Spain. Build relationships with island governors and learn to dance with their daughters at balls. Or, abandon national loyalties and become a freelance pirate. Either way, the game focuses on simple trade economics, ship and crew management, and simple naval warfare. The crew must be kept happy, healthy, and well-fed, and the ship must be kept seaworthy and armed. Gain money to maintain both ship and crew by trading goods from port to port or raiding shipping.

Challenge/Play Time: Low–moderate/Medium

Topics: Trade; financial management and economic development; sixteenth- and seventeenth-century Caribbean geography and trade routes; piracy; naval warfare. (WH 6.4; G 4, 11, 12, 13; EC 1, 2, 5, 6)

Browser-Based Games

Jamestown Online Adventure

Scripted decision-making; browser-based; (www.historyglobe.com/jamestown/)

The *Jamestown Online Adventure* is a simple simulation that allows the player to choose where to settle the English colonists of the Virginia Company, how to relate to Native Americans, what type of settlement to build, and how to generate a living. After these choices are made, the game rates the success of the player's colony. A standout feature of this otherwise quite short and simple game is the ability to consult a copy of the Virginia Company Charter with relevant portions highlighted.

Salem Witchcraft Hysteria

*Scripted decision-making; browser-based; National
Geographic (www.nationalgeographic.com)
www.nationalgeographic.com/salem*

In this game that is probably better characterized as an online narrative
experience, the player assumes the role of a Salem resident accused of
witchcraft. The player has very little control; an engaging second-person
narrative describes the player character's thoughts and experiences,
however, and effective color, font, and image choices help convey a tiny
bit of the horror of being an accused witch. Most interaction is limited
to informational links the player can select to get more background on
the historical figures of late seventeenth-century Salem. The player is given
one choice only in the game, though it makes little difference in the overall
outcome. This seems essentially to be the point the designers tried to make:
how powerless accused witches were.

Other Possibilities

Horse and Musket: Volume I

*Turn-based tactical war; multiplayer; Matrix Games
(www.matrixgames.com); $*

Like *Rise of Prussia* below, *Horse and Musket* concerns Prussia and its
opponents, but focuses on tactics using a hex-based map with units
represented as stands of miniature figures, rather than the higher level
strategic focus of the former game.

Rise of Prussia

*Turn-based military strategy; multiplayer; Ageod
(www.ageod.com); $*

Rise of Prussia is a war game focused on the Seven Years War. Developed
by Ageod, makers of *Birth of America* and *American Civil War 1861–5*, *RoP*'s
core gameplay is similar to these titles: turn-based grand strategy on a map
divided into irregularly shaped regions using units represented by tokens.

Versailles Mysteries

Adventure/exploration; Ageod (www.ageod.com); $

The player, in the role of a French noble at Louis XIV's Versailles in 1682,
attempts to solve a mystery. In the process, the player experiences the

sights and sounds, and takes part in some of the major activities of court life under the Sun King.

AMERICAN REVOLUTIONARY WAR

Birth of America

Turn-based military strategy; demo; Ageod (www.ageod.com/en/); $

Overview: In this turn-based strategic war game of the American Revolution the player takes command of the British or Rebel forces. The map is divided into regions, each with its own supply level and loyalty to the British or Rebel cause. Units are represented by individual tokens. The player sets each unit to one of a series of aggressive or defensive stances and attempts to use these units to seize control of strategic regions. Battles are resolved through calculations based on the units in each army. The game is particularly good at focusing on issues of travel and supply.

Challenge/Play Time: Moderate–high/Medium. The main challenge is to make sense of the wealth of information factored into the game: large numbers of units and regions, supply settings, the aggression stances of units, and so on.

Topics: Grand strategy and military operations in the American Revolutionary War; regional geography, political geography. (US 3.1, 3.2; G 4; EC 2)

Empire: Total War

See entry under Europe—Eighteenth Century to Napoleonic Wars

Other Possibilities

Birth of America II: Wars in America 1750–1815

Turn-based military strategy; multiplayer; Ageod (www.ageod.com/en/); $

A significantly revised and expanded version of the original *BoA* that incorporates new rules and expands the period of time covered.

EUROPE—EIGHTEENTH CENTURY AND NAPOLEONIC WARS—POLITICS AND MILITARY

Empire: Total War II

Real-time tactical battles/turn-based strategy campaign, nation-building; demo; multiplayer; Creative Assembly (www.creative-assembly.co.uk/); $ www.totalwar.com

Overview: *Empire: Total War* applies the *Total War* game model to the eighteenth century—the age of gunpowder. Players lead a nation or kingdom in Europe, Asia, North Africa, or the Americas. A secondary campaign places the player in various North American colonial military engagements up to and including war for independence against Britain. The campaign play is similar to *RTW* and *MTW*, but new elements have been introduced to the core strategy. Now players can develop a number of small towns in each province rather than simply the capital city. The player can also research scientific and technological advances. Diplomacy is expanded with more economic options included. Warfare is similar in operation to that of previous games in the series and fairly represents the look and feel of musket combat including the noises, formations, and time needed for reloading weapons.

Challenge/Play Time: Moderate challenge/Short length for an individual battle; Medium length for a partial campaign. Playing the demo or any individual battle is easier than playing the campaign.

Topics: Eighteenth-century European, African, and Asian types of infantry, cavalry, and artillery; equipment and weapons; physical geography of Eurasia; political powers of eighteenth-century Europe and world; fortifications; trade; science and technology; financial management and economic development; diplomacy. (WH 6.3, 6.4, 6.5; G 4, 8, 12, 13, 15; EC 1, 2, 5)

Europa Universalis 3

See entry under Early Modern Europe—Nation-building

Imperial Glory

Turn-based nation-building and campaigning/real-time tactical battles; Mac version available; demo; $ www.imperialglory.com

Overview: *Imperial Glory* is similar to *Empire: Total War* but focused explicitly on Napoleonic Europe, though not on Napoleon himself. The player manages the economy, building, scientific and technological research, and military aspects of a European, West Asian, or North African nation in the late eighteenth and early nineteenth century. The campaign map is divided into regions, each with a capital city. Armies move between adjacent regions like squares on a chessboard; when two opposing forces occupy the same province, a real-time battle breaks out similar to those in the *Total War* series. The portrayal of warfare is a bit more generic and simplified in *Imperial Glory* than *ETW*, but the game offers a reasonable introduction to Napoleonic warfare. Unlike *ETW*, *Imperial Glory* can be played on PCs with more modest systems, making it the winner when low system requirements are needed.

Challenge/Play Time: Moderate challenge/Short length for an individual battle; Medium length for a partial campaign. Playing the demo or any individual battle is easier than playing the campaign.

Topics: See *Empire: Total War*

Napoleon: Total War

Real-time tactical battles/turn-based strategy campaign, nation-building; demo; multiplayer; Creative Assembly (www.creative-assembly.co.uk/); $ www.totalwar.com

Overview: *NTW* is fundamentally similar to *Empire: Total War* but focused explicitly on Napoleonic Europe. Imperial management, with a focus on developing provinces, remains the same. The main changes are the introduction of troop types and organizations from the Napoleonic period and a narrative campaign that takes the player through Napoleon's military career.

Other Possibilities—Napoleonic Wars

Commander Napoleon at War

Turn-based nation-building/war; Mac version available; multiplayer; Slitherine (www.slitherine.com); $

Another turn-based Napoleonic game, *Commander Napoleon at War* also includes a research element where players can attempt to discover new military technologies for their nation.

Napoleon's Campaigns

Turn-based military strategy; multiplayer; Ageod (www.ageod.com); $

As the title suggests, this Ageod game covers the Napoleonic wars using the characteristic Ageod interface employed in *Birth of America* and *American Civil War 1861–5*.

John Tiller's Battleground Napoleonic Wars

Turn-based war; multiplayer; Matrix (www.matrixgames.com); $

An excellent turn-based, miniature-style Napoleonic game, the map is represented as a hybrid of isometric 3D topography combined with hex-based divisions. The focus is on brigade- and division-level tactics and terrain.

Browser-Based Games

Battle of Waterloo

Scripted decision-making; browser-based; BBC (www.bbc.co.uk/history/interactive/games/) www.bbc.co.uk/history/british/normans/launch_gms_battle_hastings.shtml

The mechanics of this short game are identical to those in the BBC's *Battle of Hastings*. The player takes the role of Napoleon or Wellington, chooses from one of three or four tactical options, watches the effects play out in a scripted animation, and is offered a new set of choices. After several choices are made, the battle comes to a close. Like its sibling, *Battle of*

Hastings, the game is not deep but does illustrate the basic elements of this particular battle.

Battlefield Academy: Refight Trafalgar

Turn-based war; browser-based; BBC (www.bbc.co.uk/ history/interactive/games) www.bbc.co.uk/history/ british/empire_seapower/launch_gms_trafalgar_ bfacademy.shtml

This naval variant of *Battlefield Academy* has the same top-down grid style map with simple graphics representing combatants. To move ships, the player selects each one and clicks on its destination. Ships must be next to one another to fire. Since the ships start 10+ squares apart and there are approximately 30 to control, executing a turn's worth of commands is a bit excruciating.

Battlefield Academy

Turn-based war; browser-based; BBC (www.bbc.co.uk/ history/interactive/games) www.bbc.co.uk/history/ british/launch_gms_bfacademy.shtml

See the description under Ancient World—Romans. The player must win the Roman and medieval battles to gain access to the Napoleonic battle.

EUROPE—INDUSTRIAL REVOLUTION AND NINETEENTH CENTURY

Browser-Based Games

Muck and Brass

Scripted decision-making; browser-based; BBC (www.bbc.co.uk/history/interactive/games) www.bbc. co.uk/history/british/victorians/launch_gms_muck_ brass.shtml

Muck and Brass requires the player to make key decisions about the development of an industrial city in England. Issues of sanitation and health are paramount. The game offers a quick, but reasonable overview of the impact of industrialization on English city life.

Who Wants to Be a Cotton Millionaire?

Scripted decision-making; browser-based;
BBC (www.bbc.co.uk/history/interactive/games)
*www.bbc.co.uk/history/british/victorians/launch_*
gms_cotton_millionaire.shtml

Similar in structure and presentation to *Muck and Brass*, this game focuses on managing a factory in early industrial England. As a new textile factory owner, the player makes key decisions about capital investment, labor, etc. and finds out the economic consequences of their actions. The game offers a quick, simplistic, but not unreasonable overview of factory technologies and labor practices early in the industrial revolution.

AMERICAN CIVIL WAR

American Civil War 1861–1865: The Blue and the Gray

Turn-based war (grand strategy); demo; Ageod
(www.ageod.com); $

Overview: A turn-based war game made by the developers of *Birth of America*. Gameplay is fundamentally similar to that of *BoA*: the map is divided into distinct regions, units are represented by counters and have levels of aggression, and supply is an important factor. As *BoA* does for the American Revolution, *ACW 1861–1865* offers an excellent simulation of grand military strategy in the American Civil War.

Challenge/Play Time: Moderate–high challenge/Medium length; the main challenge is to make sense of the wealth of information factored into the game: large numbers of units and regions, supply settings, the aggression stances of units, and so on.

Topics: Grand strategy and military operations in the American Civil War; regional geography, political geography. (US 5.2; G 4; EC 2)

Take Command: 2nd Manassas

Real-time tactical battles; demo; multiplayer; Mad
Minute Games (http://www.madminutegames.com); $

Overview: The player commands either the Confederate or Union army in a variety of smaller engagements related to Second Manassas, or the full battle. Play is conceptually similar to the *Total War* series in that the player gives orders to units in real-time. The player lacks the bird's eye view and extremely powerful camera of that series, however—an annoyance that nevertheless, increases the accuracy of the simulation greatly. Simulated written messages travel back and forth between the player and other officers in real time, not instantaneously. One of the great benefits of the game is the artificial intelligence. When the player is not directly controlling a unit, it will be controlled by the computer, hiding behind cover and firing as the situation demands. This illustrates reasonably well the amount of control junior officers had over their brigades and the limited control any general could exercise over the whole army beyond simple instructions.

Challenge/Play Time: Moderate challenge/Medium length; the game, like most war games, takes time to become accustomed to, but the AI assistance helps considerably.

Topics: American Civil War types of infantry, cavalry, and artillery; equipment and weapons; physical geography of Manassas battlefields, tactical warfare. (US 5.2)

Other Possibilities

John Tiller's Battleground Civil War

Turn-based tactical battles; multiplayer; Matrix (www.matrixgames.com); $

An excellent turn-based miniature style Civil War game with the map represented as a hybrid of isometric 3D topography combined with hex-based divisions. The set includes the battles of Bull Run, Shiloh, Antietam, and Gettysburg. Gameplay focuses on regimental- and brigade-level tactics and terrain.

AGE OF IMPERIALISM

East India Company

See entry under Early Modern Europe

Victoria 2

Real-time nation-building; Mac version available; demo; Paradox Interactive (www.paradoxplaza.com); $
www.victoria2.com

Another detailed and sophisticated historical simulation game from Paradox Interactive, *Victoria 2* plays like the other titles in Paradox's strategy line—

Europa Universalis and *Hearts of Iron*. In *Victoria* the player controls a country in the nineteenth century. While one can play virtually any historical country in the world from the period, the core gameplay focuses on guiding a European nation both to carve out a global empire and maintain a powerful presence in Europe.

WORLD WAR I

World War I—La Grande Guerre

Turn-based war and grand strategy; demo; Ageod (www.ageod.com); $

Overview: *World War I* is developed by the makers of *Birth of America* and *American Civil War 1861–1865*, and its core gameplay is fundamentally similar to those games. Now the region-based map and unit counters represent the struggles of the First World War. Players also conduct diplomacy and can engage in military research.

Challenge/Play Time: Moderate–high/Medium length. The main challenge is to make sense of the wealth of information factored into the game: large numbers of units and regions, supply settings, the aggression stances of units, and so on.

Topics: Grand strategy and operations in World War I; regional geography, political geography. (WH 8.2; G 4; EC 2)

Browser-Based Games

Trench Warfare

Scripted decision-making; browser-based; BBC (www.bbc.co.uk/history/interactive/games) www.bbc.co.uk/schools/worldwarone/hq/trenchwarfare. shtml

Adopting the role of a British general, the player selects the types of weapons/units and the order in which they will attack an enemy trench or defend their own. An animated sequence and a text analysis explain the results of each battle and after four battles a narrative ending is presented.

EUROPE—ROAD TO WORLD WAR II

Hearts of Iron II and *Hearts of Iron III*

Real-time nation-building, military strategy; Mac version available; demo; Paradox Interactive (www.paradoxplaza.com); $

Overview: *Hearts of Iron II* and *III* are real-time nation-building and military strategy games by the makers of *Europa Universalis*. The player controls one country in the period 1936–1945; though the nations with the largest role in the Second World War will provide some of the most detailed gameplay, one can literally lead almost any nation from the period. The game takes considerable time to learn but is an excellent simulation of grand strategy, military operations, politics, and economics in the period. (See Chapter 3 for an overview of real-time nation-building games.)

Challenge/Play Time: High challenge/Long; the tutorials are detailed and helpful, but expect to put time and effort into learning how to play.

Topics: World War II; world political, economic, and military systems 1936–1945; diplomacy, world physical and political geography 1936–1945; financial management and economic development. (WH 8.3, 8.4. 9.1; G 4, 8, 12, 13, 15; EC 1, 2, 5)

Making History: The Calm and the Storm

Turn-based nation-building, military strategy; Muzzy Lane Software (http://www.muzzylane.com); $ http://making-history.com/

Overview: *Making History* offers a nation-building experience similar to *Hearts of Iron*. Play is turn-based rather than real-time, though players engage in similar activities of diplomacy, financial management, and warfare. The multiplayer mode is the best aspect of the game, allowing players to compete over a network as leaders of rival nations. There are two versions of *Making History*. The first was originally designed as an educational simulation. The revised "commercial game" version, however, took complicated gameplay and simplified it significantly; it warrants serious consideration for classroom use.

Challenge/Play Time: Medium challenge/Medium length–long

Topics: See *Hearts of Iron*

Browser-Based Games

Battle of the Atlantic (BBC)

Scripted decision-making; browser-based;
BBC (www.bbc.co.uk/history/interactive/games)
www.bbc.co.uk/history/worldwars/wwtwo/
launch_gms_battle_atlantic.shtml

Serve as a British naval officer assigned to lead Allied ships through waters filled with German submarines. Start by learning naval tactics and techniques in "school" (a series of text and graphic lessons). Then lead a convoy to safety, by making key tactical decisions along the route.

Battlefield Academy (BBC)

Turn-based war; browser-based; BBC (www.bbc.co.uk/
history/interactive/games) www.bbc.co.uk/history/
british/launch_gms_bfacademy.shtml

See the description under Ancient World—Romans. The player must win the Roman, medieval, and Napoleonic battles to gain access to the Second World War battle.

COLD WAR

Tropico 3

City-building, nation-building; demo; Kalypso Media
(www.kalypsomedia.com/en-us/); $
www.tropico3.com

Overview: *Tropico 3* provides an interesting twist on the city-builder genre. The player takes the role of dictator, "El presidente" in the game world, of a generalized Spanish-speaking island in the Caribbean that evokes associations with Cuba. The daisy chain economy and world of inhabitants with specific needs and wants are all in play. The simulation of life as a dictator is reasonably detailed. The player controls wages, in addition to the hiring and firing of workers. The player also can issue edicts, craft speeches, and terrorize opponents. One of the key concerns of the player is to achieve his goals while maintaining sufficient support from one or more key constituencies on the island, groups ranging from nationalists and religious proponents, to environmentalists and capitalists.

Challenge/Play Time: Moderate challenge/Medium length. The game itself is equivalent in its difficulty to any other city-builder at its core, but the variety of political and economic options exceed those in other city-builders. The tutorial provides a very good overview of basic gameplay, speeding the process of learning the game considerably.

Topics: Political operations; totalitarianism; government methods of controlling a populace; unrest in totalitarian regimes; financial management and economic development; mid-twentieth-century Caribbean architecture; urban geography, urban planning, and urban systems; trade; production of goods. (WH 9.1; G 12, 14, 15; EC 1, 2, 3, 5, 15, 16)

Other Possibilities

Freedom Fighter '56

Roleplay/adventure; Lauer Learning
(www.lauerlearning.com); $
www.freedomfighter56.com
Described by its developers as an "interactive graphic novel," *FF '56* depicts a group of Budapest freedom fighters attempting to end the oppressive regime that ruled Hungary in 1956. Play focuses on the dynamics of street protests and government repression.

CROSS-PERIOD GLOBAL

Civilization III and IV, FreeCiv

Turn-based nation-building; Mac version available;
Firaxis (www.firaxis.com); $ (except FreeCiv)
Civilization: www.civilization.com
FreeCiv: www.freeciv.net
Overview: These are all versions of the classic turn-based game of civilization-building referred to throughout this book. Found a late Neolithic city and grow a civilization that reaches to new planets. *Civilization III* was released in 2001 and re-released in 2005—it is older but still highly playable and able to run on computers with very modest systems. *Civilization IV* came out in 2006 and *Civilization V* was released in 2010. *FreeCiv* is a freely available clone of the original *Civilization* game from 1990—it is no match for the commercial versions, but its price and extremely low system requirements make it an option.

UNITED STATES—POST 1945

Politics

Political Machine (2008)

Turn-based political strategy; demo; Stardock Games (www.stardock.com/); $
www.politicalmachine.com

Overview: Manage a general election campaign for the U.S. presidency. Develop an electoral strategy and implement it by traveling to critical states and emphasizing key political messages through a variety of media.

Challenge/Play Time: Low challenge/Short length. The core gameplay is simple enough that the basics can be communicated in a few minutes and play can begin.

Topics: U.S. presidential elections; campaign strategies; key political issues of early twenty-first-century U.S. voters. (US 10.1, 10.2; EC 1, 2, 16)

Other Possibilities

Capitalism 2

Economic management; demo; Enlight (www.enlight.com); $
www.enlight.com/capitalism2

As the title implies, the player attempts to build a successful business that can outperform its rivals in the free market. As CEO of the company, the player decides, among other issues, the goods to manufacture, advertise, and sell, the managers to keep, and those to replace.

Democracy 2

Turn-based political strategy; Positech (www.positech.co.uk); $
www.positech.co.uk/democracy2

Attempt to lead a democracy composed of citizens with different and often opposing interests. Manage taxes, crime, climate change, and a host of other issues by setting policies and seeing the results.

Browser-Based Games

The Redistricting Game

Turn-based political strategy; browser-based; USC Annenberg
www.redistrictinggame.org
Players act as consultants for state legislators trying their hand at redistricting voters. The game explores the effects redistricting can have on the balance of political power and the ability of state legislators to achieve goals.

MODERN CITIES

City Life (2007) and *City Life 2008*

City-building; CDV Software (www.cdvusa.com); $
citylife.cdvusa.com
Overview: *City Life* is a city-builder set in a modern Western society. Beyond the standard challenges of managing finances, traffic, pollution and other components of urban life, the player must balance the desires of various socio-economic groups ranging from the fringe to the elite and the working class.
Challenge/Play Time: Moderate challenge/Short–medium length. A good tutorial exists that leads players gradually through the basic steps of play
Topics: Urban planning, urban management; social dynamics; needs of city dwellers.

Energyville (Chevron)—See entry under Contemporary Global Issues—Environmental Issues

SimCity Societies (2007)

City-building; demo; Electronic Arts (www.ea.com); $
simcitysocieties.ea.com
Overview: *SimCity: Societies* offers a different variant of city-building, one that allows players to explore cities focused on specific social philosophies and values. Players can construct buildings that reflect

and increase or decrease the level of social values ranging from authoritarianism and productivity, to spirituality and creativity. The appearance of the city shifts over time to reflect the social values with the highest levels. This allows players to consider basic connections between socio-political philosophies, urban spaces, and architecture.

Challenge/Play Time: Moderate challenge/Short–medium length. A good tutorial exists that leads players gradually through the basic steps of play.

Topics: Urban planning, urban management; political and social philosophies; needs of city dwellers.

CONTEMPORARY GLOBAL ISSUES

Against All Odds

Turn-based life management/refugee simulation; various gameplay; browser-based; United Nations High Commissioner for Refugees (www.unhcr.org/cgi-bin/texis/vtx/home)
www.playagainstallodds.com

Developed for the United Nations Commission on Refugees, this Flash game attempts to show players a glimpse of the difficulties refugees face when forced to flee their homes and attempt to build a new life. Note that there are depictions of state-sanctioned violence against individuals that may be disturbing to some viewers.

Ayiti: The Cost of Life

Turn-based life management; browser-based;
Global Kids (www.globalkids.org)
ayiti.newzcrew.org/ayitiunicef

Ayiti is a powerful simulation of the hardships endured by a family living in poverty in Haiti. The player must identify a goal for the family of five (money, happiness, health, education) and attempt to reach that goal over 4 years. Core gameplay involves considering how to balance the need for income with the desirability of getting an education and the health-damaging hardships of unskilled labor. The game is frustrating in the best sense: it is difficult to make ends meet for the family.

Climate Challenge

Turn-based nation-building; browser-based;
BBC (www.bbc.co.uk) www.bbc.co.uk/sn/hottopics/
climatechange/climate_challenge

Take the role of the leader of the European Union for the twenty-first century, empowered to make critical decisions at the national and local level concerning trade and industry, household energy consumption practices, etc. Available actions are represented as cards that can be played. Each card has costs and benefits expressed in terms of greenhouse gas emissions, food, water, energy, and wealth. Each action also has a certain level of voter popularity associated with it. It is the goal of the player to manage the EU economy successfully and promote prosperity while reducing carbon emissions. A game of trade-offs, *Climate Challenge* presents the complex difficulties surrounding reducing greenhouse gases very well.

Consumer Consequences

See below; browser-based; American Public Media
(americanpublicmedia.publicradio.org)
sustainability.publicradio.org/consumerconsequences

Really a survey, not a game, but the ability to choose the face, hair, clothing, and accessories of the player's avatar, the appealing design, and the changes in the environment based on the answers given to the questions make *Consumer Consequences* feel game-like, in the best sense. The player answers a series of questions about her lifestyle and a tally is kept of how many earths would be required to sustain the earth's population if everyone lived like the player. This is a must try. It is simple, engaging, and highly provocative about the impact of lifestyles in developed nations.

Darfur is Dying

Life management; browser-based;
mtvU (www.mtvu.com) www.darfurisdying.com

A "narrative simulation" of the experiences of refugees in Darfur developed at the USC with the sponsorship of mtvU, the Reebok Human Rights Foundation, and the International Crisis Group. Players attempt to gain water and food and eke out a living without falling prey to the militias that range the land. This effort raises the questions of whether and how to simulate issues of this level of gravity, but, at the very least, it may raise awareness—a very good thing. Note that the subject matter of the game may be very disturbing to some.

Energyville

Turn-based city-builder; browser-based; Chevron
(www.chevron.com)
www.willyoujoinus.com/energyville

Energyville tasks the player with establishing the sources of power for a city of the future. Players decide the percentages of the city's power demands to supply by sources including fossil fuels, solar and wind power, nuclear energy, biomass, and hydro-power. Each power source has associated costs, environmental impact, and security issues. After selecting the necessary power sources, the game projects the success of the player's energy policy over a several year period. At the end of two turns the player's overall energy score is calculated and can be compared to those of previous players.

A Force More Powerful

Turn-based political management; York Zimmerman
(www.yorkzim.com); $
www.afmpgame.com/

Organize, manage, and conduct a nonviolent protest strategy against a regime. Manage resources, assign different characters and groups to key leadership roles and attempt to change or replace the regime. The designers clearly hope that AFMP can serve as an inspirational model, though not a how-to guide, for real-world nonviolent protests.

Peace Maker

Turn-based nation-building; Impact Games
(www.impactgames.com); $

Acting as either the president of Palestine or prime minister of Israel, the player attempts to negotiate a lasting peace within their term of office. Efforts are impeded by continued misunderstandings and acts of outright violence on both sides.

Real Lives 2010

Turn-based life management; demo; Educational
Simulations (www.educationalsimulations.com); $

A global lifestyle simulator, *Real Lives 2010* assigns the player to guide a newborn person living in a place and set of economic circumstances that are chosen randomly from myriad global possibilities. Play consists primarily of setting goals and making basic strategies for the player's avatar then pressing the "age a year" button and seeing how those strategies play out. The game is a wealth of information containing statistics on the family's economics, wealth, lifestyle, etc.

Stop Disasters

Turn-based city-builder (of sorts); browser-based; UN International Strategy for Disaster Reduction (http://www.unisdr.org/) www.stopdisastersgame.org/en/
Protect a village or city from disasters like floods and tsunamis by using sound construction techniques and taking steps to prevent and minimize the effects of catastrophic weather.

Third World Farmer

Turn-based life management; browser-based www.3rdworldfarmer.com
Make the farming and household decisions for a family in a hypothetical developing nation (ostensibly in Africa, though there seems to be some conflation of Asian issues—for example, the player can be offered the option of growing opium). Plant crops, attempt to earn enough to survive and even thrive. A series of challenges ranging from droughts to civil wars hamper the player's ability to keep his family healthy.

TYPICAL COURSE OUTLINES AND LISTS OF AVAILABLE GAMES

To help with planning, these outlines take the games listed in the profiles above and organize them so that teachers can see at a glance the games that are currently available for the various units of three commonly taught courses: World History, Western Civilization, and U.S. History. The headings for the World History and U.S. History units come from the voluntary national history standards from the National Center for History in the Schools:

* http://nchs.ucla.edu/standards/us-standards5-12.html
* http://nchs.ucla.edu/standards/world-standards5-12.html

The unit headings have not been included for eras that currently have few or no games available for them.

After the name of each game is a genre tag in parentheses:

NB   nation-building
NB/W   nation-building/war
CB   city-builder
T   trade
W   war
PM   political management
LM   life management
SDM   scripted decision-making
A   adventure

In addition, browser-based games include a BB.

World History

Early Civilizations and the Emergence of Pastoral Peoples, 4000–1000 BCE

Egypt
History Egypt: Engineering an Empire (NB)
Immortal Cities: Children of the Nile (CB)

Classical Traditions, Major Religions, and Giant Empires, 1000 BCE–300 CE

See entries below under Classical World/Axial Age—Rome

The Emergence of the First Global Age, 1450–1770

1701 AD (CB)
Civilization: Colonization (NB)
East India Company (T)
Port Royale 2 (T)
Sid Meier's Pirates (T)

An Age of Revolutions, 1750–1914

Empire: Total War (NB/W)
Horse and Musket (W)
Rise of Prussia (W)

A Half-Century of Crisis and Achievement, 1900–1945

Hearts of Iron (NB)
Making History (NB)

The Twentieth Century since 1945: Promises and Paradoxes

Against All Odds (SDM)
Climate Challenge (PM)
Darfur is Dying (LM)
Freedom Fighter '56 (A)
A Force More Powerful (PM)
Peace Maker (NB)
Real Lives 2010 (LM)
Stop Disasters (M)
Third World Farmer (LM)
Tropico 3 (CB)

World History across the Eras

Civilization (NB)

Western Civilization

Classical World, Axial Age c. 600 BCE–500 CE

Rome

Battlefield Academy (W; BB)
Caesar IV, CivCity: Rome, Grand Ages Rome (CB)
Emperor of Rome (SDM; BB)
Europa Universalis: Rome (NB)
Glory of the Roman Empire (W)
Rome: Total War (NB/W)

Medieval Europe c. 500–1450 CE

XIII Century (W)
Battle of Hastings (W; BB)
Battlefield Academy (W; BB)
Dawn of Discovery (CB)
The Guild 2 (RP)

Medieval: Total War 2 (NB/W)
Stronghold 2 (CB)
Viking Quest (SDM; BB)

Early Modern Europe c. 1450–1700

Europa Universalis (NB)
Patrician (T)
Versailles Mysteries (A)

First Global Age c. 1450–1750

1701 AD (CB)
Civilization: Colonization (NB)
East India Company (T)
Port Royale 2 (T)
Sid Meier's Pirates (T)

Eighteenth-Century Nation-Building

Empire: Total War (NB/W)
Europa Universalis (NB)
Horse and Musket (W)
Rise of Prussia (W)

Napoleonic Era

Battle of Waterloo (W; BB)
Battlefield Academy (W; BB)
Battlefield Academy: Refight Trafalgar (W; BB)
Commander Napoleon at War (W)
Imperial Glory (NB/W)
John Tiller's Battleground Napoleonic Wars (W)
Napoleon: Total War (NB/W)
Napoleon's Campaigns (W)

Nineteenth-Century Industrial Revolution and Imperialism

Muck and Brass (SDM; BB)
Who Wants to Be a Cotton Millionaire? (SDM; BB)

World War I and Russian Revolution

Trench Warfare (W; BB)
World War I—La Grande Guerre (SDM,W)

Interwar Period, Nazism, Fascism, Totalitarianism, Second World War

Battle of the Atlantic (W; BB)
Battlefield Academy (W; BB)
Hearts of Iron (NB)
Making History: The Calm and the Storm (NB)

Modern World Post-1945

Against All Odds (LM)
Climate Challenge (PM/NB)
Freedom Fighter '56 (A)
Tropico 3 (CB)

U.S. History

Three Worlds Meet (Beginnings to 1620)

Civilization: Colonization (NB)
Medieval: Total War 2 Gold Edition (contains sixteenth-century America's expansion) (NB/W)

Colonization and Settlement (1585–1763)

1701 AD (CB)
Civilization: Colonization (NB)
Jamestown Online Adventure (SDM; BB)
Salem Witchcraft Hysteria (SDM; BB)

Revolution and the New Nation (1754–1820s)

Birth of America and *Birth of America II* (W)
Empire: Total War (NB/W)
Europa Universalis (NB)

Civil War and Reconstruction (1850–1877)

American Civil War 1861–1865: The Blue and the Gray (W)
John Tiller's Battleground Civil War (W)
Take Command: 2nd Manassas (W)

Postwar United States (1945–early 1970s)

Tropico 3 (CB)

Contemporary United States (1968–present)

Capitalism 2 (T)
City Life (CB)
Democracy 2 (PM)
Energyville (CB; BB)
Political Machine (PM)
The Redistricting Game (PM; BB)
SimCity Societies (CB)

Logistical Considerations

Time Requirements, Software, and Hardware

DETERMINING HARDWARE AND SOFTWARE REQUIREMENTS

Desktop Games

Before committing to a particular desktop game (as opposed to a game that is played in an Internet browser, about which, see below), it is necessary to ensure that the hardware and software needed to play the game are available. Talk to the school's tech specialist or department to determine the specifications of the school's computers. System requirements for games are regularly displayed somewhere on the outside of the game box, usually on the back or one of the sides. The arrangement can be listed as a set of independent bullet points or as categories with headers. Usually both minimum and recommended system requirements are provided. The distinction, as the terms suggests, is between the hardware the game absolutely must have to be playable and what it needs to run at moderate quality. If the game is played on a machine that only meets the minimum requirements, players may need to lower the performance settings of the game (usually found in the options section of the game's main screen)—manuals and online guides can assist in this if the effect of the options settings is insufficiently clear.

The system requirements for *Medieval II: Total War*, a game published in 2006, provide an example of a system requirements entry one might find on a game box, see Table AB.1.

Dawn of Discovery, a city-builder published in 2009, provides a second example, see Table AB.2.

Table AB.1

Minimum system requirements	Recommended system requirements
Windows 2000/Windows XP	2.4 GHz Intel Pentium 4
1.5 GHz Intel Pentium 4	1 GB RAM
512 MB RAM	17 GB of uncompressed hard drive space
17 GB of uncompressed hard drive space	256 MB NVidia GeForce 7300 or greater or ATI Radeon X1600 or greater
Direct X 9.0c compliant 128 MB video card with hardware acceleration and pixel shader 1.0 support	
Direct X 9.0c compatible 16-bit soundcard and speakers or headphones	
4X DVD-ROM drive	
Windows compatible mouse and keyboard	

Table AB.2

Supported OS	Windows XP/Windows Vista
Processor	Pentium 4.3 GHz or comparable (dual core recommended)
RAM	512 MB RAM
Video card	Direct X 9.0 compatible graphics adapter with 128 MB RAM (DirectX10 with 512 MB recommended)
Sound card	Direct X 9.0 compatible
DVD-ROM	DVD-ROM Drive
Hard drive space	6 GB
Peripherals supported	Windows-compliant mouse, keyboard, gamepad, headset

There is no standard way to display system requirements for a game. There are standard items of information, however, that any legitimate system requirement listing will include. These are:

Operating System

The computer operating systems upon which the game will run. For Windows games of the past decade the operating systems include (from earliest to most recent) Windows 2000, Windows XP, Windows Vista, and Windows 7. Games designed for earlier versions of Windows *may* run on more recent versions. The reverse is not true; games designed for later operating systems will generally not run on earlier ones. Windows 7 generally runs both XP and Vista games fine, though this is not always the case. It is imperative that the version of the game that will be used by the school be installed and tested on the school's computers to ensure it will run.

Processor

The CPU (central processing unit) of the computer. Intel is the primary manufacturer of CPUs for PCs. The great variety of Intel processors available and their general abilities are a bit complicated to follow. Essentially, there are two facets of a processor's rating. The first is the chip itself. For Intel these are the most likely chips to be listed on system requirements since 2000 in general order of the performance of the chip from lowest to highest.

- Pentium III
- Pentium 4
- Core Duo
- Core 2 Duo
- Core 2 Quad
- Core i7

To make matters more complicated, AMD also manufactures processors for Windows-based machines. When using computers with AMD processors, talk to a tech professional, do some online research, or contact technical support for AMD or a particular game manufacture to determine what Intel processor is comparable.

The second facet is the speed of a processor, currently listed in GHz (gigahertz). The larger the number is, the faster the chip. These two facets combine to make a great number of variants within each chip category. As of 2010 some of the newest games are taking advantage of dual and quad core processors; most games, however, will run on a Pentium 4. The higher up the scale the processor is, generally, the better the performance (speed, smoothness of graphics, responsiveness of controls, etc.) of the game. This means that, for practical purposes, the processor, particularly if it is at least a Pentium 4 of 3 GHz speed or better, will run a game if all the other necessary system requirements are met.

Memory

Memory is a far easier category to decipher; it refers to the total main memory the computer has. Memory for Windows PCs is currently measured in GB (gigabytes). Make sure that the computers have at least the amount of memory listed in the system requirements; more memory may make the game run better.

Hard-drive Space

Most consumer hard drives are measured in GB, though there are affordable drives available with terabytes of capacity (1 terabyte, TB, ≈ 1,000 GB). The hard-drive requirement for a game is the amount of space the game needs to store its essential files.

Video Card

For video games of the past decade, the most important system requirement is the video card, the piece of hardware responsible for rendering a game's graphics. There are two main brands of video cards: NVidia and ATI. Certain games will run only on one or the other, but more often, games run on both brands of card, so long as the card has sufficient built-in video memory. Video card memory as of 2010 is generally measured in MB (megabytes), though cards with 1GB (1GB ≈ 1,000 MB) of video memory are becoming increasingly common. Games made before 2005 will generally run on a 64 MB card, though some require 128 MB. Games after 2005 generally require a 128 MB card; the most graphically intensive games of 2008–2010 require 256 MB cards, and recommendations (though not requirements) for 512 MB cards are just beginning to appear for a few games in 2010. Historical strategy games, fortunately, often do not require the most advanced graphics.

Some computers, especially laptops but also more modestly priced desktops, use an integrated video processor, i.e. one that is an integral part of the main computer motherboard, not a separate, specialized video card. The most commonly used is the Intel Integrated graphics processer. Integrated video uses RAM from the computer's main memory supply as opposed to a dedicated video card, which has its own built-in memory. Depending on the speed of the computer's processor and the amount of main RAM, integrated graphics processors can run a number of simulation games effectively. They pose two drawbacks, however. First they offer lower performance than video cards. Second there is no easy conversion between the amount of RAM an integrated card has access to, and a corresponding dedicated video card. Generally speaking an integrated graphics card will often perform as a low end version of a dedicated card that has an equivalent amount of dedicated RAM, but this is far from a guarantee.

CD-ROM/DVD-ROM

Digitally downloadable, diskless, copies of software are becoming more common, but many, if not most, games are still purchased on physical disks. Current games tend to require a DVD drive to be read; before 2005, most games required only CD-ROM drives to play.

Macintosh System Requirements

Far fewer games run on Macintosh computers than PCs, though more do now that all Macintoshes have Intel processors. The key system requirements in a typical Macintosh game listing are essentially the same as for a Windows computer: operating system, processor, memory, disk space, video card, and DVD drive. As far as video cards go, NVidia and ATI are still the dominant brands for Macintosh. The main differences when reading system requirements for Macs are the operating system and processor possibilities. OS X ("10") is the operating system that has been included with new Mac computers since 2002. There are many versions of OS X and each follows the numbering convention of three integers separated by periods where the second and third number run from 0 to 9, so that, for example, 10.3.2 is a more recent version than 10.2.8. The other critical difference is that Macs made before 2006 can have PowerPC processors rather than Intel processors. Since almost all simulation games are made for Windows-based PCs first, which have Intel processors, and later converted to be run on Macs, Macs with Intel processors are able to run a greater variety of game software than older Macs with PowerPC processors.

Regardless of how closely a school's computers appear to meet the system requirements for a particular game, whenever possible the best course is to test a demonstration (demo) version of the game on the computers, before purchasing full copies. Many games are promoted by free demo versions that allow players to experience core gameplay and see how the game runs on their particular systems before committing to a purchase. When the demo runs successfully, the full game almost certainly will. Still, it is always safest to go one step further and install and test the full games before using them in the class. Most games will install and play without a hitch. Some, however, may require extra tweaking to run smoothly on particular computers.

Browser-Based Games

There are a number of web-based simulation games available, particularly dealing with current global issues. These games by far offer the easiest point of entry into using simulation games. They are free, generally take no more than 30 minutes to play (and sometimes considerably less), and operate essentially on all modern web browsers, which are freely available on the web in both Windows and Macintosh versions. The vast majority of web-based games run on the Flash player, a free and nearly ubiquitous plug-in that adds multimedia capabilities to web browsers for both PCs and Macs. The newly released iPad does not currently support Flash; whether this will change remains to be seen. A few older games run on the Shockwave player, a predecessor to Flash. The major limitation of Internet games is connection speed. Computers with slower connections will need additional time to download web games. Generally speaking, any form of high speed connection will suffice, though faster connection speeds will result in shorter waiting times.

Even if the game is browser-based, it is a good idea to test the game out on the actual computers that will be used—if a computer does not have the Flash plug-in installed, for example, it will not be able to play a Flash game. These are issues that can easily be rectified if identified ahead of time. Not taking the time to plan ahead, however, can result in unhappy surprises for a teacher.

DETERMINING THE NUMBER OF COMPUTERS NEEDED

Often the number of computers to be used is simply the number available. It is not always the case, however, that a teacher should employ every computer at their disposal. When planning for the necessary computers, there are several significant factors to consider:

- How many students will be playing the games?
- How many computers and copies of the game are available for the students?
- Will all students play the same game?
- Will game playing sessions take place during class, outside of class, or some combination of the two?

An optimal classroom set-up will generally have one computer with the game installed to every two or three students; if games are to be played as homework, students will need to have computers with their own installed copies of the game or access to a computer lab at school outside of class time.

Even when optimal conditions cannot be met, however, there are many solutions to incorporate video game-based lessons using a modest amount of equipment. At one extreme, effective game-based lessons can be conducted using one computer and a screen projector. In such a configuration, the teacher or a skilled student plays the game while the rest of the class offers input and makes observation notes. Real-time strategy games that offer a great number of moving parts to observe, such as many city-builder games or a particular battle in a war game, lend themselves to this sort of use. There are even advantages to doing so. When the game remains under the teacher's control, students can focus on observing and commenting on the game without needing to learn to play; a great deal of time can be saved this way when the game is only needed to provide a brief simulation experience. More details on running these kinds of lessons can be found in the next chapter.

With a bit more technological know-how—a colleague, savvy student, or local tech guru can help here—one can also use a freeware recording utility such as Fraps (www.fraps.com) to record a gameplay session, then replay the video in class for observation and discussion. If a computer lab is small, students can work in groups larger than three, taking turns playing, observing, and sharing their insights with peers. For practical purposes, groups of larger than three are difficult to accommodate at a single computer; two or three students are most effective. These are guidelines, however, not absolutes.

BUDGETING FOR AND ACQUIRING GAMES

The cost of commercial games is a potential barrier that needs to be met creatively. New copies of current games can be expensive. Fortunately, there are a variety of solutions to keep costs down. Using demos when possible is a cost-effective way to introduce commercial simulation games to the class. They generally contain a tutorial and enough play time to serve for a classroom lesson. For example, *Total War* demos each contain a complete historical battle; the *East India Company* demo provides a simple model of naval combat from the eighteenth century and a 10-year-long session of play in the main trading game (about 30 minutes); and the *Political Machine* demo enables players to conduct 10 weeks of a presidential campaign. Demos such as these can provide enough content for a teacher interested in providing a short experience with a simulation. Another strategy is to have the students play demos but purchase a few copies of the full game for interested students to play at greater length.

Unless there are compelling reasons to shop in local retail stores—a school has the resources, or only purchases its software from certain places—far better bargains can be found online than in brick-and-mortar stores. Retail department stores and electronics chains will carry the best-selling games, but they will tend to charge premium prices for them even when the games themselves are a year or more old and can be obtained far less expensively elsewhere. Online game retailers tend to offer the best deals. Amazon.com often offers an excellent balance of low price, extensive inventory, and convenience for those who want to purchase hard copies of games, i.e. the actual game disks. There are also growing numbers of digital distributors, which allow consumers to purchase the rights to download and install digital copies of games. The recognized leader in this market is currently Valve Software's Steam (www.steam.com); Stardock's Impulse (www.impulsedriven.com) and Direct2Drive (www.direct2drive. com) are also both currently reasonable options. If slow Internet speeds are not an issue, these companies offer the ability to purchase, download, and install games very quickly. This is not always a viable solution for school use, however, unless the service provides site licenses to cover multiple computers using the same downloaded copy or the school is able to set up a purchaser's account for each computer. Currently, site licenses for commercial games are not common, but, hopefully, over time more digital distributors will adopt this business model.

Special mention should be made of the online service Good Old Games (www.gog.com). Good Old Games, started in 2009, sells directly downloadable games that are at least 5 years old and span as far back as the first half of the 1990s. Each game is tested and updated as needed to play on current versions of Windows operating systems. This is a terrific resource for purchasing digital copies of older but still very useful simulation games.

LEARNING TO PLAY FOR YOURSELF

Before making a proposal to school administrators and requesting technical and financial support, indeed before committing to a simulation for classroom use, it is critical that a teacher become familiar with the game they intend to use in the class. In other words, they need to learn how to play the game. Consider the criterion for a useful simulation game, the ability to offer defensible explanations of cause and effect in the past. Whether a game does this to the necessary standards of a teacher cannot be determined if the teacher does not play the game. The situation is analogous to the use of any other resource for learning. No teacher should ever assign a text to be used in class that they have not read, or a movie that they have not seen. The same principle holds true for games. As we shall see in the next chapter, the teacher using simulation games is responsible for making sure that students successfully learn how to play the game. This is difficult to achieve at best if the teacher is unfamiliar with the game. There is also a larger philosophical issue here. Teachers cannot rightly expect their students to take on the challenges of learning to play and analyzing a simulation game if the teachers themselves are unwilling to do so.

There are a number of forms of support a teacher can draw upon when learning to play a game. One of the best is to ask a student who is experienced with playing strategy games to help the teacher learn the game. This provides a great opportunity to empower a student to help out by sharing expertise that is all too often ignored in typical classrooms. Many games have online support in the form of discussion forums, official websites, wikis, and even how-to videos on YouTube created by loyal fans. Typing the title of the game into a web search engine should yield a large number of results. Several key terms can be added to narrow the search:

- *FAQ*: Frequently asked questions. These documents are often written in question-and-answer format and can deal with general issues of gameplay to very specific tutorials.
- *Walkthrough*: A step-by-step guide to playing and completing a given game.
- *Strategy guide*: As the name suggests, a guide to various successful strategies that can be employed in a game.

A demo version also provides an excellent opportunity for the teacher to assess the difficulty of the game, the content in the game, and the historical issues raised by the game.

PROPOSING THE SIMULATION TO ADMINISTRATORS

Ultimately, any proposal for using simulation games in a history class should be based upon a teacher's thoughtful consideration of the points from the past three chapters. For sake of convenience, the list below covers the main points to review and consider when making a written or oral proposal for simulations to administrators. Above all, be prepared. Consider the following points as examples of the types of issues that may need to be discussed and be ready to answer questions.

1   Consider the general benefits of simulations as learning tools and the talking points discussed at the end of Chapter 1.
2   Make sure to do your homework and select a game or games that will mesh well with the curricular objectives for the unit or class in question. Be able to articulate how the game does this.
3   Describe the genre of the game and note its appropriateness for the age group in question.
4   Confirm ahead of time that the school's computer resources are sufficient to support the simulations in question. Identify multiple suppliers and prices for the games. Before doing so, however, it is a good idea to find out whether the school has an exclusive purchasing relationship with one or more vendors for software.

It is always a good idea to provide options and be willing to start small. Consider the following hierarchy of costs and commitment:

1   Implementing a simulation-based lesson using web-based games in a school lab with computers that are already connected to the Internet requires administrators only to support your efforts at innovative teaching for one class period and allocate time for your class in the lab.
2   Lessons involving free computer demos also come with no financial involvement, though some tech support will be needed to install the software. These games may take longer to play but can still be limited investments of time.
3   Lessons that require fewer copies of games or older games will generally be less expensive to fund than those requiring newer games and more copies.

Demonstrating that you have thought through the necessary steps carefully, are willing to be flexible in your approach, and appreciate the need for financial responsibility will go a long way in persuading administrators to support your efforts.

Resources for Web Publishing

There are several free options available for publishing student blogs and other writing on games on the Internet. Depending on the needs of the class, options are available that restrict viewers of the publications to those with login credentials, or make the writing of the class available to anyone on the web. It cannot be stressed enough, however; be sure to obtain approval from your school administrators before publishing student writing on the web.

BLOG SITES

WordPress (www.wordpress.com) is one of the best known providers of blogging software and hosting space for blogs. The basic service is free and allows a user to create a blog site with a personalized URL. Site access can be open to anyone or restricted to invited users making it an effective option for private class work. Writing to the blog is simple and writers can include graphics, organize content in a variety of ways, and receive comments from recognized viewers. The following books offer an introduction to using Wordpress.

- *WordPress Bible* by Aaron Brazell (Wiley).
- *WordPress: Visual Quick Start Guide* by Jessica Neuman Beck and Matt Beck (Peachpit Press).
- *WordPress For Dummies* by Lisa Sabin-Wilson (For Dummies).

Google Blogger (www.blogger.com) is the other leading provider of blogging software and hosting space. Like WordPress, Blogger offers a variety of features and options to users including the ability to limit access to the site. For more information on Blogger, visit the site or consider the following books:

- *Google Blogger For Dummies* by Susan M. Gunelius (For Dummies).
- *Publishing a Blog with Blogger: Visual Quick Project Guide (2nd Edition)* by Elizabeth Castro (Peachpit Press).

MOODLE AND COURSE MANAGEMENT SYSTEMS

For schools that maintain their own servers, a superior option for taking advantage of the ease and flexibility of online publishing and communication is a course management system. A CMS provides the software to develop an online component to any class with options ranging from digital submission of assignments and online quizzes, to blogs, forums, and chats. If your school does not have a content management system, Moodle (moodle.org) is an established, stable, and free open source CMS that can be installed on a school's servers. Moodle provides the full range of online communication and publishing options, but has the additional advantage of being hosted on your school's servers, an advantage when trying to secure privacy for students' offerings. For more information, visit the site. There are many books available about designing online courses with email. Two good starting points are:

- *Moodle Teaching Techniques: Creative Ways to Use Moodle for Constructing Online Learning Solutions* by William Rice (Packt Publishing).
- *Moodle 1.9 E-Learning Course Development: A complete guide to successful learning using Moodle* by William Rice (Packt Publishing).

Further Reading and References

GENERAL TWENTY-FIRST-CENTURY EDUCATIONAL ADVOCACY, THEORY, AND SKILL SETS

There are a number of recent books discussing the critical skill sets of the twenty-first century. One can get a good introduction by surveying the following works:

- H. Gardner, *Five Minds for the Future*, Boston: Harvard Business Press, 2008
- D. Pink, *A Whole New Mind*, New York: Riverhead Books, 2005.
- T. Wagner, *The Global Achievement Gap*, New York: Basic Books, 2008.

Gardner is the well known author of the theory of multiple intelligences and approaches these issues from a cognitive perspective, while Pink and Wagner's approaches are more from a business/entrepreneurial angle.

Both the National Council for Social Studies and the National Council for Teachers of English have issued position statements on twenty-first-century media literacy:

- NCSS Position Statement on Media Literacy, www.socialstudies.org/positions/medialiteracy
- National Council for Teachers of English, *21st Century Literacies*, www.ncte.org/positions/21stcenturyliteracy

THE DISCIPLINE OF HISTORY AND HISTORICAL THINKING—COGNITION IN HISTORY AND HISTORY EDUCATION

When it comes to studying the core of historical thought and the difference between how experts and students think about history, one can do no better than to start with S. S. Wineburg, *Historical Thinking and Other Unnatural Acts*, Philadelphia, PA: Temple University Press, 2001. For the original articles that provide the core for much of this work, see S. S. Wineburg, "Historical Problem Solving: A Study of the Cognitive Processes Used in the Evaluation of Documentary and Pictorial Evidence," *Journal of Educational Psychology*, 1991, vol. 83, pp. 73–87; and Wineburg, "On the Reading of Historical Texts: Notes on the Breach between School and Academy," *American Educational Research Journal*, 1991, vol. 28, pp. 495–519.

A number of important journal articles have treated the issue of historical problem solving in the wake of Wineburg's initial studies in the early 1990s. See, K. T. Spoehr and L. W. Spoehr, "Learning to Think Historically," *Educational Psychologist*, 1994, vol. 29, pp. 71–77. For an extension of these principles to middle school, see B. A. VanSledright, "Fifth Graders Investigating History in the Classroom: Results from a Researcher-Practitioner Design Experiment," *The Elementary School Journal*, 2002, vol. 103, pp. 131–160; see also B. A. VanSledright, "Confronting History's Interpretive Paradox while Teaching Fifth Graders to Investigate the Past," *American Educational Research Journal*, 2002, vol. 39, pp. 1089–1115.

There are a number of excellent essays on the historical craft that illuminate the inherent subjectivity in the history while not succumbing to nihilism and abandoning the discipline altogether. Though close to 50 years old, the discussion of "The Historian and His Facts" is still a terrific place to start; see E. H. Carr, *What Is History?*, New York: Vintage Books, 1961, pp. 3–35. See also A. Schlesinger, "History: Text vs. Context," *Proceedings of the Massachusetts Historical Society*, Third Series, 1991, vol. 103, pp. 1–8; C. Larmore, "History and Truth," *Daedalus*, 2004, vol. 133, pp. 46–55; an excellent survey of the development of history as a field over the centuries comes from J. H. Arnold, *History: A Very Short Introduction*, Oxford: Oxford University Press, 2000.

RELEVANT RESEARCH INTO LEARNING AND PEDAGOGY

The most recent survey of the field of learning theory and pedagogy as it applies to classroom teachers can be found in A. Bransford, A. Brown, and R. Cocking (Eds.), *How People Learn*, Washington, D.C.: National Academy Press, 1999. This book, among many other ideas, notes the importance of teaching students how experts in a discipline approach problem-solving, an idea promoted also by R. J. Sternberg, "What Is an Expert Student?" *Educational Researcher*, 2003, vol. 32, pp. 5–9.

There are a number of good recent articles on the benefits and challenges of multimedia learning, though these tend to focus more on the fields of science and mathematics. See, for example, R. Moreno and R. E. Mayer, "Cognitive Principles of Multimedia Learning: The Role Of Modality And Contiguity," *Journal of Educational Psychology*, 1999, vol. 91, pp. 358–368; R. E. Mayer, P. Mautone, and W. Prothero, "Pictorial Aids for Learning by Doing in a Multimedia Geology Simulation Game," *Journal of Educational Psychology*, 2002, vol. 94, pp. 171–185; G. B. Semb and J. A. Ellis, "Knowledge Taught in School: What Is Remembered?" *Review of Educational Research*, 1994, vol. 64, p. 277. R. E. Mayer's article, "Should There Be a Three Strikes Rule Against Pure Discovery? The Case For Guided Methods of Instruction," *American Psychologist*, 2004, vol. 5, pp. 14–19, is particularly important in its warning that teachers must not remove themselves from discovery learning sessions, but remain present as expert guides for students.

A helpful exploration of digital and face-to-face discussion for students comes from J. Guiller, A. Durndell, and A. Ross, "Peer Interaction and Critical Thinking: Face-to-face or Online Discussion?" *Learning and Instruction*, 2008, vol. 18, pp. 187–200.

SIMULATIONS AND MICROWORLDS IN SCIENCE AND MATHEMATICS EDUCATION

The role of microworlds in science and mathematics education has been the subject of a fair amount of research worth examining for its applicability to history and social studies education.

See, for example, J. M. Monaghan and J. Clement, "Algorithms, Visualization, and Mental Models: High School Students' Interactions With a Relative Motion Simulation," *Journal of Science Education and Technology*, 2000, vol. 9, pp. 311–325; B. White and J. R. Frederiksen, "Inquiry, Modeling, and Metacognition: Making Science Accessible to All Students," *Cognition and Instruction*, 1998, vol. 16, pp. 3–118; L. P. Steffe and H. G. Wiegel, "Cognitive Play and Mathematical Learning in Computer Microworlds," *Educational Studies in Mathematics*, 1994, vol. 26, pp. 111–134; R. Moreno, R. E. Mayer, H. A. Spires, and J. C. Lester, "The Case for Social Agency in Computer-Based Teaching: Do Students Learn More Deeply when They Interact with Animated Pedagogical Agents? *Cognition and Instruction*, 2001, vol. 19, pp. 177–213; M. Kordaki, "The Effect of Tools of a Computer Microworld on Students' Strategies Regarding the Concept of Conservation of Area," *Educational Studies in Mathematics*, 2003, vol. 52, pp. 177–209.

VIDEO GAMES AND LEARNING

The seminal work in the field of games and learning comes from J. P. Gee, and readers interested in learning about general games and learning theory should start with his books, *What Video Games Have to Teach Us about Learning and Literacy*, New York: Palgrave Macmillan, 2003; and *Good Video Games and Good Learning*, New York: Peter Lang, 2007. See also D. W. Shaffer, *How Computer Games Help Children Learn*, New York: Palgrave Macmillan, 2006. Important work has been done in the journals, and the following articles offer good points of introduction to the field: R. Garris, R. Ahlers, and J. Driskell, "Games, Motivation, and Learning: A Research and Practice Model," *Simulation and Gaming*, 2002, vol. 33, pp. 441–467; H. F. O'Neil, R. Wainess, and E. L. Baker, "Classification of Learning Outcomes: Evidence from the Computer Games Literature," *The Curriculum Journal*, 2005, vol. 16, pp. 455–474; K. Squire, H. Jenkins, W. Holland, H. Miller, A. O'Driscoll, K. P. Tan, and K. Todd, "Design Principles of Next-Generation Digital Gaming for Education," *Educational Technology,* 2003, vol. 43, pp. 17–23; S. McLester, "Game Plan," *Technology and Learning*, 2005, vol. 26, pp. 18–26; S. Tobias and J. Fletcher, "What Research Has to Say About Designing Computer Games for Learning," *Educational Technology*, 2007, vol. 47, pp. 20–29. For a counterpoint to these studies, R. Clark, "Learning from Serious Games? Arguments, Evidence, and Research Suggestions," *Educational Technology*, 2007, vol. 47, pp. 56–59. Be sure to read Squire's response to Clark in K. Squire, "Games, Learning, and Society: Building a Field," *Educational Technology*, 2007, vol. 47, pp. 51–55.

FORMAL ANALYSIS OF VIDEO GAMES

Alongside the work on games and learning has arisen a parallel literature analyzing games as works of media. Some see games as a form of narrative, others as rule-based systems that should not be analyzed as narratives; there are myriad opinions in between. The best way to learn about the variety of viewpoints, ideas, and issues among the formal analysts of games is to browse the articles in the three-part series by N. Wardrip-Fruin and

P. Harrigan: *First Person: New Media as Story, Performance, and Game*, Cambridge, MA: MIT Press, 2004; *Second Person: Role-Playing and Story in Games and Playable Media*, Cambridge, MA: MIT Press, 2007; and *Third Person: Authoring and Exploring Vast Narratives*, Cambridge, MA: MIT Press, 2009. Monographs on the analysis of games include: J. Juul, *Half Real: Video Games Between Real Rules and Fictional*, Cambridge, MA: MIT Press, 2005; I. Bogost, *Persuasive Games: The Expressive Power of Videogames*, Cambridge, MA: MIT Press, 2007; I. Bogost, *Unit Operations: An Approach to Videogame Criticism*, Cambridge, MA: MIT Press, 2008;

C. Elverdam and E. Aarseth, "Game Classification and Game Design: Construction Through Critical Analysis," *Games and Culture*, 2007, vol. 2, pp. 3–22; K. Salen and E. Zimmerman, *Rules of Play: Game Design Fundamentals*, Cambridge, MA: MIT Press, 2003.

SERIOUS GAMES

For a thorough analysis of serious games, see I. Bogost, *Persuasive Games*, Cambridge, MA: MIT Press, 2007. For considerations of serious games from the design perspective, see D. Michael and S. Chen, *Serious Games: Games That Educate, Train, and Inform*, Boston: Thomson Course Technology, 2006; and N. Iuppa and T. Borst, *Story and Simulations for Serious Games: Tales from the Trenches*, Burlington, MA: Focal Press, 2007.

NEW MEDIA LITERACY

For recent examples of guides to reading and writing in the Internet age, see R. Beach, C. Anson, L. Kastman Breuch, and T. Swiss, *Teaching Writing Using Blogs, Wikis, and Other Digital Tools*, Norwood, MA: Christopher Gordon, 2008; see also M. B. Eagleton and E. Dobler, *Reading the Web: Strategies for Internet Inquiry*, New York: Guilford Press, 2007.

Some Sources on the Web for Research Assignments

HISTORICAL DOCUMENT COLLECTIONS

- Center for History and New Media, *World History Sources* (chnm. gmu.edu/worldhistorysources/).
- Paul Halsall, *Internet History Sourcebooks Project* (www.fordham.edu/ halsall/).
- Yale Law School, *Avalon Project: Documents in Law, History, and Diplomacy* (avalon.law.yale.edu/).
- Kathryn Talarico, *ORB: The Online Reference Book for Medieval Studies* (http://the-orb.net/).
- Center for History and New Media, *Liberty, Equality, Fraternity: Exploring the French Revolution* (chnm.gmu.edu/revolution/).
- Tufts University, *Perseus Digital Library* (www.perseus.tufts.edu/ hopper/).
- Ibis.Com, *Eyewitness to History—History Through the Eyes of Those Who Lived It* (www.eyewitnesstohistory.com/).

NEWS MAGAZINES WITH ONLINE FULL TEXT ARTICLES

The following news magazines (and there are many others) have full-text articles available on their websites and searchable indices.

- *Newsweek* (www.newsweek.com/).
- *The Economist* (www.economist.com/).
- *U.S. News and World Report* (www.usnews.com/).
- *Time* (www.time.com/time/).

UNITED NATIONS AND OTHER GOVERNMENT INFORMATION SITES

- World Food Programme (www.wfp.org/).
- UNICEF (www.unicef.org/).
- UNHCR (High Commission on Refugees) (www.unhcr.org/).
- *CIA World Factbook*, online (www.cia.gov/library/publications/the-world-factbook).

PUBLIC BROADCASTING SITES WITH EXTENSIVE HISTORICAL RESOURCES

- BBC History (www.bbc.co.uk/history/).
- PBS History (www.pbs.org/history/).

LIBRARIES WITH EXTENSIVE ONLINE CONNECTIONS

- U.S. Library of Congress Digital Collections and Services (www.loc.gov/library/libarch-digital.html).
- British Library Online Gallery (www.bl.uk/onlinegallery/index.html).

MAP COLLECTIONS

- David Rumsey Historical Maps Collection (www.davidrumsey.com/).
- UT Perry Castañeda Library Map Collection (www.lib.utexas.edu/maps/).

Games and Learning

Web Resources

Many groups are involved in researching the learning potential of games, and the educator who is serious about games and learning may want to keep an eye on the field. There is always a risk that websites will be abandoned over time, so this appendix lists only a few of the most established sites. For future updated lists, visit the author's site, Historical Simulations in the Classroom (historicalsimulations.org).

EDUCATION ARCADE (WWW.EDUCATIONARCADE.ORG)

A cutting-edge group of researchers and scholars centered on MIT dedicated to studying the ability of games to foster meaningful learning both informally and in formal educational contexts. A number of important scholars in the field collaborate with TEA.

GAMASUTRA (WWW.GAMASUTRA.COM)

The primary site on the web devoted to the concerns of professional game programmers and designers. Gamasutra is maintained by Think Services, which also operates the seminal Game Developer's Conference and publishes the industry magazine, *Game Developer*. Gamasutra is the place to go for the latest editorials, information on games, and insights into all facets of game design and development.

GAMES FOR CHANGE
(WWW.GAMESFORCHANGE.ORG)

G4C promotes the ability of games to speak to the problems of the world. In addition to editorials and resources, G4C has an extensive, searchable database of serious games that can be accessed through the website and played.

GAMES, LEARNING, AND SOCIETY
(WWW.GAMESLEARNINGSOCIETY.ORG)

A cutting edge academic and industry group like the Education Arcade, Games, Learning, and Society is based at the University of Wisconsin–Madison. GLS pursues the study of games as learning tools in formal and informal educational contexts.

SIMULATING HISTORY
(SIMULATINGHISTORY.COM)

A Canadian group of academic researchers who are, as their website puts it, "exploring the 'best potential' for educational computer simulations to teach Canadian history."

WATER COOLER GAMES
(WWW.BOGOST.COM/WATERCOOLERGAMES)

Water Cooler Games is the site of Ian Bogost, a prolific and insightful theorist about video games as media, and a founder of the Persuasive Games studio. The site is primarily a large scale blog of Bogost's ideas, but contains a wealth of ideas and information about the serious games field in addition to links to a number of serious games.

SERIOUS GAMES SOURCE
(WWW.SERIOUSGAMESSOURCE.COM)

This is the Think Services companion site to Gamasutra, and devoted to the coverage of serious games. Like Gamasutra, the site focuses on offering current editorials on all matters related to serious games.

References in the Text

Diamond, Jared, *Guns, Germs, and Steel*, New York: W. W. Norton, 1997.

Gee, J. P., *Good Video Games and Good Learning*, New York: Peter Lang, 2007.

Guiller, J., Durndell, A., and A. Ross, "Peer Interaction and Critical Thinking: Face-to-face or Online Discussion?" *Learning and Instruction*, 2008, vol. 18, pp. 187–200.

Salen K., and E. Zimmerman, *Rules of Play: Game Design Fundamentals*, Cambridge, MA: MIT Press, 2003.

Index

Note: only games referred to in the text substantially are listed in the index.

See Appendix A for a more thorough list of current historical simulation games.